8 $\frac{75}{N}$

IN THE MARGIN OF HISTORY

IN THE
MARGIN OF HISTORY

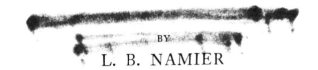

BY

L. B. NAMIER

Essay Index Reprint Series

 BOOKS FOR LIBRARIES PRESS
FREEPORT, NEW YORK

First Published 1939
Reprinted 1969

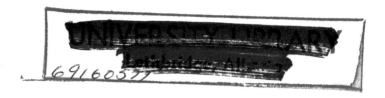

STANDARD BOOK NUMBER

8369-0050-2

LIBRARY OF CONGRESS CATALOG CARD NUMBER

69-18934

PRINTED IN THE UNITED STATES OF AMERICA

PREFACE

MOST of the essays in this book have been printed before, and are now republished with a minimum of change; in the case of the political essays their original dates should therefore be noted.

My best thanks are due to the editors, owners, and publishers for permission to reproduce the essays; to those of " Palestine and Middle East " for the diagram on the " Palestine Vanishing Trick "; to Sir Max Beerbohm for the cartoon of Count Berchtold and to Mr. Siegfried Sassoon who owns it; and to Flight-Lieutenant R. G. Sims, R.A.F., for the photograph of T. E. Lawrence.

L. B. NAMIER

15 GLOUCESTER WALK
LONDON, W.8
June 1, 1939

CONTENTS

FOREIGN AFFAIRS

JUDAICA

UNDER THE GEORGES

CONTENTS

FOREIGN AFFAIRS

B

DIPLOMACY, SECRET AND OPEN

("*The Nineteenth Century and After*," *January* 1938)

THERE would be little to say about " Diplomacy, Secret and Open," were it not for the nonsense which is talked about it. Diplomacy is " the organized system of negotiations between sovereign States," and in its nature and methods does not differ essentially from other kinds of negotiations. As Lord Hervey wrote, two centuries ago, the transactions between men, great and small, are

> still the same game, and played with the same cards, the disparity in the skill of gamesters in each equally great . . . the only difference is their playing more or less deep, whilst the cutting and shuffling, the dealing and the playing, is still the same whether the stakes be halfpence or millions.

But games are not played with open cards, and negotiations, whether between States, business firms or individuals, can seldom, if ever, be conducted in public.

At the root of most of the nonsense

talked about secret diplomacy lies confusion between aims and methods, between " policy " and " negotiations." The vital distinction between the two is stressed by Mr. Harold Nicolson, one of the most articulate experts and best-informed writers on diplomacy. " Policy should be subjected to democratic control: the execution of that policy should be left to trained experts." " Policy should never be, and need never be, secret "; but the conduct of negotiations must be confidential. In other words, what the public has a right to know is the general trend of national policy and any binding commitments incurred in its name; while the decision as to the amount of information to be given out about negotiations, and the choice of time for doing so, must be left to those entrusted with their conduct.

Publicity destroys the freedom of negotiations. Every word said in public is apt to commit the negotiator. This makes him over-cautious and leaves little scope for tentative proposals. Could even a non-political treaty — *e.g.* a commercial agreement — be discussed in public? At every turn " vested interests " would be created which would hamper the further course of the negotiations. Still worse where frontiers are concerned: that between the Irish Free State and Ulster admits of obvious improvements; but all thought of such amendments, which could have been made

4

on a basis of give and take, had to be dropped because of the vested interests created by the treaty once it was published. Those included in the State in which they wish to be, even if less numerous, have a moral superiority in asserting the *status quo* over those who would profit by a change.

In fact, premature publication, or " exposure," is a well-known method of interfering with negotiations. When in the spring of 1919 an inter-Allied Committee suggested a frontier which would have satisfied very nearly the maximum of Polish territorial claims against Germany, their secret report speedily found its way into the French Press, it being hoped by those who committed the indiscretion that the intense anti-German feeling in Allied countries would henceforth preclude any material change in the proposed frontier. There was a great deal to be said for that frontier which gave Danzig to the Poles, but not for the attempt to put pressure on what ought to have been a quasi-judicial body, considering territorial claims in the light of certain acknowledged principles; and the attempts of decent negotiators to find just solutions are seldom helped by public discussion and agitation. The fruit will be poor if prematurely plucked by incompetent and irresponsible hands, and orchards therefore require a reasonable measure of protection and seclusion.

There is a further, very important, reason why

DIPLOMACY, SECRET AND OPEN

diplomatic negotiations must be conducted in secret. Most nations are extremely touchy. " National honour " and " national prestige " were a fetish in this country in the eighteenth century, and are still on the European Continent; and the less honour nations observe in practice, the more sensitive are they to anything which might seem to question what amount of it they possess. The British and French Governments must have repeatedly charged the Italians with breach of faith in the matter of non-intervention in Spain, even before Mussolini proudly proclaimed it to the world, and must have hinted at what everyone knew about the nationality of the pirate submarines in the Mediterranean. But any such public pronouncement originating from our side would have rendered further negotiations impossible.

Altogether, the veil thrown over a great deal of diplomatic transactions, in so far as this country is concerned, often serves the purpose of hiding from the British public the bad manners and unreasonable nature of foreign Governments; in other words, it serves the interest of peace. Otherwise damage is apt to occur. The Kruger telegram, which was a public act, is a case in point. It did serious and lasting harm to Anglo-German relations and weighed heavily with public opinion in this country. But in diplomatic intercourse

with the Germans such incidents are by no means
rare. What reception would the Kaiser have received from the British public in 1899 had they
known that he had refused to accept the invitation
of his grandmother unless the British Government
first gave way to his petulant and unreasonable
demands arising out of some obscure squabbles in
Samoa? Again, had every step in the negotiations for a limitation of naval armaments been
disclosed to the British public, Sir Edward
Grey's policy would have been fully justified in
their eyes, but further talks would have become
impossible.

Generally speaking, the public and the Press
are much more inflammable than professional
diplomats, or even Cabinet Ministers, who have
to consider the consequences of " blowing off
steam." Mr. J. A. Spender, an unimpeachable
witness, thus describes the position during the
years preceding the Great War:

> The game as played by the diplomats
> required secrecy, and, so long as the game
> went on, its dangers were limited by exclud-
> ing an audience which must have taken sides.
> What a Foreign Secretary feared in nine
> cases out of ten was not the craft of his
> opponent but the too zealous backing of his
> own side, which would have cut off his re-
> treat. Keep the public out of it, and it was

a relatively safe game; let the public in, and
it instantly became full of deadly peril. As
a rule the public were only let in when the
Foreign Secretary or his Government had
decided not to retreat.

Still, those who are keenest on " open diplomacy " also favour " diplomacy by conference."
If only statesmen met and had heart-to-heart talks!
Then they would see that there was something to
be said on the other side, and each would find that
the other is not such a bad chap after all. And
if they meet and the public see them in the daily
Press so nicely together, their faces wreathed in
smiles, it feels that here is " open diplomacy " —
not that sinister exchange of secret notes between
Foreign Offices. The hearts of the public soften,
and so apparently do the brains. For nothing can
beat, or even equal, the secrecy of such meetings:
what the two statesmen say often remains hidden
from their own competent official advisers, from
their colleagues in the Cabinet, and sometimes
even from these two men themselves; after such a
talk, each knows best what he himself has said, or
what he had meant to say, or what he wishes he
had said, but has only a dim and blurred recollec-
tion of what the other man said, or tried to say.
Seldom has there been such a talk which, if put to
the test, did not produce a crop of fatal disagree-

ments as to what had been agreed upon; witness, *e.g.*, the interview between Aehrental and Isvolsky at Buchlau, which led to the Bosnian crisis, the forerunner of the Great War. Even where such interviews do not result in misunderstandings, they very seldom produce positive results. It is in the interest of decent diplomacy and of international comity that every step should be carefully examined and considered, that neither side should feel that it has been " had," or that it has unduly yielded to charm and persuasion. Surprising results or gains obtained in personal interviews can seldom be maintained afterwards; in August 1906, at Björkoe, the Kaiser obtained what he desired from the Tsar, but the Russian Foreign Office soon managed to back out of that absurd agreement. Even mutually advantageous treaties, if the product of a cordiality between statesmen which is not shared by their nations, are likely to do more harm than good. The Thoiry agreement between Briand and Stresemann is an outstanding example; they reached a complete understanding, and were both promptly disavowed by their countries.

As Mr. Nicolson says, diplomacy, to be effective, " should be a disagreeable business." Diplomatic negotiations should be conducted with calm clearness and with hard-headed perseverance — best of all on paper; even then there is room for

9

differences in interpretation, but infinitely less than in the case of verbal agreements. Nor is there in written negotiations the same inducement to make undue concessions. To quote Mr. Nicolson again: " There is nothing more damaging to precision in international relations than friendliness between the Contracting Parties "; the difficulties of precise negotiations in conference arise " from the more amiable qualities of the human heart," from " consideration, affability or ordinary good manners," and from the " human difficulty of remaining disagreeable to the same set of people, for days on stretch."

None the less, personal contacts and conversations are at times essential, just because they offer that measure of freedom and elasticity which secrecy alone can secure; diplomatic notes have their own publicity, with posterity and history. But then personal negotiations had better not be conducted by the principals, but much rather by officials or juniors. What these suggest or listen to commits nobody; they can explore every approach and discuss all kinds of schemes. In the fifteenth century Phillippe de Commynes wrote in his " Memoirs," when commenting on a meeting between Louis XI and Charles the Bold:

Et deux grans princes qui se vouldroient
bien entreaymer ne se devroyent jamais veoir,

mais envoyer bonnes gens et sages les ungs
vers les autres, et ceulx-la les entretiendroient
ou amanderoient les faultes.

Meetings between juniors or officials cannot produce the dilemma of their Governments having
either to accept an unsatisfactory arrangement or
to disavow a man who is supposed to have the
power to enter binding agreements. The fatal
mess of the Hoare-Laval agreement could never
have arisen had the matter been transacted through
ambassadors, or even through the Permanent
Under-Secretary without the Minister. As Mr.
Nicolson says, " the execution of policy should
be left to trained experts."

Even so, the Foreign Secretary needs to be to
some extent an expert, perhaps more so than any
other Cabinet Minister. The best British Foreign
Secretaries by preference limited themselves to
that one sphere: Castlereagh, Canning, Pal-
merston, Salisbury, Sir Edward Grey. It is
dangerous for ordinary politicians to handle international negotiations. In the first place, their
attention is too much divided between the public
at home, which they are accustomed to watch, and
the interests which ought to be the paramount
consideration of foreign policy. Further, there
is the vanity of politicians, connected with their
habit of playing to the gallery. Lastly, there is

the danger of their failing to make the necessary readjustments. Some succumb to the delightful atmosphere of diplomatic courtesy; accustomed for years to the rough and tumble of the House of Commons, they are apt to accept the courtesies of diplomatic life at their face value, and to mistake the form for substance. Mr. Snowden, on the other hand, very nearly produced a serious breach with the French at the Hague by treating them as he was wont to treat the " right hon. gentlemen opposite "; after the scene caused by his use of the word " grotesque," he remarked, slightly perturbed, to one of his assistants: " But surely I have not said anything unparliamentary? "

Still, while the Foreign Secretary should understand the methods and traditions of diplomacy, he ought to be thoroughly free of foreign fancies. There is, in the first place, the question of foreign languages. No man is lightly to be chosen for the post of British Foreign Secretary who speaks any language but English; or at least, a man burdened with such accomplishments should be made to take a vow never to speak any other language. He is certain not to know every foreign language which matters; and if he is familiar only with one, he tends to develop an undue bias in favour of that particular nation. But if, worst of all, he prides himself on such knowledge, and finds pleasure in jabbering that foreign lingo, then he is lost and essential British interests are in jeopardy. Lord Salisbury knew French, but never talked anything but English to foreign statesmen or diplomats.

Lastly, a statesman dealing with international affairs should know nothing about " Teschen." He cannot know every Teschen on the map, and if he knows one Teschen only, it will hide whole worlds from his sight; and even about the Teschen with which he happens to be acquainted, he will probably know less than his experts, and his information about it will, in most cases, be out of date. A Foreign Secretary had much better possess a knowledge of Continents pleasantly blended with an ignorance of particular foreign countries, and allow himself to be informed by his experts when occasion arises. These he must know how to choose. Judgment of men, of their character, minds, and knowledge, is an essential attribute in statesmen.

The same is true of democracies; here everything depends on the choice they make of statesmen. The essence of " democracy " is that the nation should have the power to choose and change its rulers, and that it should, at all times, enjoy full freedom of political discussion. But when Mr. Harold Nicolson says that foreign policy " should be subjected to democratic control," he uses language which lends itself to misunderstanding and misinterpretation. It is difficult to see how policy can be democratically controlled, except through Parliament, and through the influence which the prevailing atmosphere exercises on Parliament and on the Cabinet. For what is public opinion, and how can it be ascertained? Or even could it be ascertained, its commands would mostly be vague and contradictory, and therefore impracticable. It would, *e.g.*, direct the Government to defend the cause of righteousness and to preserve peace; to make an omelette without breaking eggs. And even the intervention of the House of Commons (apart from the influence and pressure which it potentially exercises all the time) is dangerous. For it is in its very nature fitful, and therefore irresponsible. Once more: what the public is called upon to do is to choose its rulers, and what it is entitled to know is the general trend of national policy and any binding commitments incurred in its name.

As a rule, no commitments should be incurred which are not dictated by the national interest, and seldom, if ever, should a nation be made to promise things which it would not do without the promise. In 1919 Great Britain and America offered France a joint guarantee of her eastern frontier in lieu of a virtual French annexation of the left bank of the Rhine. When America refused to honour President Wilson's promise, Mr. Lloyd George took advantage of the clause

14

which made the British guarantee conditional on America's participation. This was wrong, even politically, for we could never afford to see France broken and the Germans in control of the Channel ports. Our frontier is the Rhine. We concede nothing in guaranteeing the security of France beforehand, and a good deal could have been done at that early stage to calm French apprehensions by giving them such a guarantee.

In 1914 a certain school of pacifists professed to detect the origin of the war in our *entente* with France and in alleged secret military and naval commitments entered into by Great Britain. In reality the war broke out over the Yugo-Slav fears of the Habsburg Monarchy and its Balkan policy; and if there was a contributory cause in Western Europe, this was to be found in the German hope that we would remain neutral — in other words, not in the existence, but in the uncertainty of our commitments to France.

Still, even whilst the foreign policy of a nation is uncertain and badly defined, contingent military and naval arrangements must be precise. Therefore, when public opinion coloured by sentimental pacifism, as ours was before 1914 and before 1936, is timid and unwilling to face realities, military and naval agreements must necessarily exceed the diplomatic commitments. A modern war cannot be undertaken like a picnic; you do not drive out in your car till you find a nice spot where you stop and have lunch. Unless precise arrangements for common action are made beforehand, chaos ensues, followed by defeat, for which the service men are made to bear the blame. In 1914 our fleet was concentrated in the North Sea, and the French in the Mediterranean; and this arrangement, which was a matter of common notoriety, amounted to a quasi-alliance, closer than was thought at that time. Sir Edward Grey made it known on August 2, 1914, that, even if we remained neutral, we would oppose a German fleet coming " into the Channel, or through the North Sea to undertake hostile operations against French coasts or shipping." Such a lop-sided neutrality might have been possible in a short war; but could Germany have put up with it once supplies from overseas acquired decisive importance? Still, without this concentration of fleets and division of responsibilities, our naval armaments would have had to be much greater, which would again have displeased and distressed the pacifists. There is no escape from this dilemma: so long as there are bullies in the world, even the most pacific nation has to seek security in armaments and alliances; and if it is unwilling to assume the commitments inherent in alliances, it has vastly to increase its own armaments.

Pacifists reply to this by paeans on the beauty

of multilateral treaties against the aggressor, whoever he may be, and of " collective security." There was, indeed, much delight and self-congratulation in this country over the noble impartiality of the Locarno Treaty. This was a splendid instrument, so long as there was no occasion for it. We could simultaneously guarantee Germany against French aggression, when it was clear that the French would not attempt another Ruhr, and France against German aggression, when the Germans had no army. But would such double engagements be possible once things have become serious?

Those who inveigh most violently against " secret diplomacy " favour " diplomacy by conference," the worst of all secret diplomacies; and, while similarly inveighing against " secret commitments," favour commitments so vague and wide as, in fact, to render their precise meaning (if they have any) secret. Never was a worse secret commitment entered into by those responsible for British foreign policy than the Covenant of the League of Nations; which, moreover, was passed by Parliament practically without discussion, as a mere appendix to the Treaty of Versailles, and under its cover. It is true the terms of the Covenant were public, and, indeed, every pacifist jazz band blared them to the world. But how many people truly understood the meaning of those commitments, and the burden which they entailed if honestly carried out, or their futility and dishonesty if that burden was shirked? Under the Covenant we were no longer entitled to restrict ourselves to the defence of our own vital interests. And those who insisted on our assuming such extensive commitments, at the same time achieved a one-sided disarmament of this country. Personally I never believed either in the League of Nations or in "collective security";[1] and immediately after the experience offered by Vilna in 1920 I put down my objection in this simple theorem: "Those who are interested cannot be impartial, while those who are not interested cannot be effective. How, then, can you have international action?" Were we prepared to go to war over Vilna, Corfu, Manchukuo, or Abyssinia? Are we prepared to go to war over Spain or China, or shall we always find shelter behind the adverse vote of some Albania or Portugal? If unanimity and true collective action is required at every step, the League will remain what it is — a sham, a miserable farce. If majority rule is adopted, it will become a deadly danger. But this is unthinkable. And even within the sphere of " economic sanctions," League action has been found more difficult and cumbrous than had been expected, and has

[1] A very different thing from a Defence Front directed against a bully who threatens all who are within his reach (April 1939).

proved ineffective because it was timid: no one wanted to go such a length as would threaten war.

The so-called " old diplomacy " was accused of dividing the world into two camps, which was said inevitably to lead to war. And where are we now? — with Germany, Italy, and Japan outside the League, allied and more aggressive than any nation dared to be before the war, but leaving their satellites in the League, presumably in order to complete its farcical discomfiture. The only effective measure of an international character, recently carried through, was the Nyon Agreement, which was concluded by one group of Powers, outside the framework of the League. And if there is any salvation for decency and liberty in the world, it is not in the Covenant of the League, dishonoured and disgraced, nor in the " splitting of articles " at Geneva, but in co-operation between Great Britain, the United States, and France, a group to which other Powers could adhere, or with which they could co-operate.

The greatest danger in foreign politics lies in what Mr. Nicolson once described as " complacent, unctuous, and empty rectitude "; in high-sounding shams which deprive people of a sense of responsibility, in a pacifism which will not face facts, and thereby hands over all power to those who count only with facts and with a capacity to create them. The last line of defence for the

League of Nations is to claim that the idea is fine, only people will not carry it out honestly. Clearly the difficulty is in men and their nature. But what is the value of a practical political programme if it is not adjusted to the real conditions of life? Those who could work the scheme of the League require no Covenant, and those for whom the Covenant is required will not work it.

There is the old, well-known story about the man who, during the Lisbon earthquake of 1755, went about hawking anti-earthquake pills; but one incident is forgotten — when someone pointed out that the pills could not possibly be of use, the hawker replied: " But what will you put in their place? "

PATHOLOGICAL NATIONALISMS

(" *Manchester Guardian*," *April 26, 1933*)

DISILLUSIONED friends of Germany are inclined to blame the Treaty of Versailles for the rise of Hitlerism. Whether that treaty was as bad as it is painted, or whether a reaction against its obvious mistakes and sympathy for the " under-dog " have carried us too far in condemning it; whether the French policy has greatly contributed to the present crisis, or whether it was based on an understanding of the German mentality sounder than our own — the bearing of the peace settlement on recent developments in Germany should not be overrated. The rise of a pathological nationalism ten or fifteen years after a national defeat seems a r current phenomenon, practically independent of the terms imposed on, or accorded to, the defeated country. It comes apparently when the children of the war period attain the age of twenty to thirty; adults may learn the lessons of war and defeat, but those who have experienced the passions of war and the bitterness of defeat while still incapable of critical understanding seem burdened with frantic, almost insane resentments, which break forth in after-life and give a pathological turn to their politics.

The Peace Treaty which closed the twenty-three years of the Revolutionary and Napoleonic wars left the national territory of France intact; the Franco-German frontier of 1815 coincides with that of 1919. None the less, about 1830 these terms were described as a " wrong " and a " disgrace," and the Bourbons, who in the peculiar circumstances of 1814–15 had been able to preserve France from real disaster, were talked of almost as the so-called " Marxists " are now in Germany. Even so, the French nationalist movement assumed generous forms and brought men of culture to the fore; but that no attempt was made at overthrowing the peace settlement of 1815 was merely due to the knowledge that such an attempt would have been met by a reconstituted Coalition of 1815.

The Boulanger movement, which swept France during the years 1885–89, bears certain curious resemblances to that of the Nazis. The nation, in search of a saviour, contrived to believe, with a well-nigh religious fervour, in a man devoid of real distinction. In the decisive moment that man, though borne by a powerful wave of popular enthusiasm, refused to transgress the limits of legality, just as Hitler did when this would have implied revolutionary action. From that moment

Boulanger was doomed; he had become ridiculous in the eyes of a nation with a tradition of bold leadership.

Probably the most generous settlement ever made after a war is that embodied in the Union of South Africa — which did not prevent the rise of a bitter nationalism about ten to fifteen years later. The same thing has happened in Ireland in De Valera's victory over Cosgrave.

In short, if my thesis is correct, a wave of nationalist exasperation was bound to sweep Germany about this time, even had the terms of the Peace Treaty been different. All loss of territory, be it only of undoubtedly French, Polish, and Danish districts, would have been described as a grievous " wrong," while the loss of Germany's dominant position in Europe, coming after four years of victories and conquests, would have been resented, as the " wound of Waterloo " was after the Napoleonic wars. Besides, it is significant and characteristic that the Nazis should now [April 1933] turn with peculiar anger against their inoffensive, " Nordic," neighbour, because of the frontier rectification in Slesvig, which is undeniably just, and which, in 1866, the victorious Bismarck had himself promised to make.

But if, in addition to the pathological reaction after defeat, any other outstanding cause is to be

23

assigned for the rise of Hitlerism, it is the economic crisis, with its concomitant unemployment, unprecedented in size and duration; were Germany in the midst of an economic boom, the present outburst would certainly not have come with the same force or assumed so savage a character. Here those obsessed by " Versailles " will perhaps interject a word about reparations. But other countries besides Germany have suffered, and still suffer, from the consequences of reparations and war debts without plunging into a Nazi " revolution "; and anyhow no financial settlement will restore the Russian and Chinese markets, or do away with Asiatic industrial competition, or offer a solution for the problems of " technocracy."

But in what sense has there been a revolution in Germany? Was it against foreign dominion? The Germans waited until the foreign armies had completed the evacuation of German territory. Was it against a despotism that denied the Nazis constitutional access to power? That road was wide open to them, and while professing contempt for Parliament the Nazis worked and waited for success at the polls. It was not a determined, impatient minority, exasperated by chaos and inertia, which seized office. Hitler went to Hindenburg and asked for " the power of Mussolini "; and when refused, said he could

PATHOLOGICAL NATIONALISMS

wait, being so much younger — a very curious
declaration for a revolutionary hero to make.
But after all the power of the State had been
peacefully handed over to him, then, and only
then, he proclaimed a " revolution." Of this the
unique feature is that lawlessness and outrages
are enacted by a Government which has obtained
power in a constitutional manner, had it confirmed
by a general election, and has met with no resistance whatever from opponents, docile towards
those in authority as only Germans can be.
Violence is all that it has in common with revolution, of which the name is only claimed as a cover
for acts of brutality and for a disregard of human
rights.

Other revolutions opened with humanitarian
ideas, with generous impulses, and magnificent
dreams; and it usually required civil war and the
fear of foreign intervention to engender terrorist
passions. The present German revolution has
dreamt no dreams, has made terrorism and sup-
pression precede resistance, and, with regard to the
rights of the individual, to Parliamentary Government, the Press, education, etc., has, by its free
and deliberate choice, adopted from the outset all
that was most ruthless in the advanced stages of
other revolutions. Shirts and salutes borrowed
from Italy and a " four years' economic plan "
imitating Russia complete the equipment of that

" national revolution," while the persecution of German Jews, who have fought and worked for Germany, is its only original contribution. History supplies no analogy for that lifeless but horrible counterfeit of revolution.

GERMAN ARMS AND AIMS

(" *Manchester Guardian*," *June* 28, 1935)

THERE is a vague belief in people's minds that Germany's face and hand are against Russia. Hitler himself asserts it, indeed, he bawls it into the world; and the Bolsheviks, convinced on principle that the " capitalist world " is scheming their destruction, accept his word. Moreover, recent experience has proved once more that an aggressive policy against the East is for Germany easier of achievement and more profitable than action against the West. But Germany's immediate neighbour and hereditary enemy in the East is Poland, and the most painful consequence of Germany's defeat is the amputation of her Polish provinces; while Russia has long been Prussia's ally, and should be even more so now that the previous community of interests, based on spoils, has been replaced by a community of suffering. Before 1933 the recovery of the lost territories in the East was the foremost objective of every nationally minded German. But Hitler has made friends with the Poles. This *volte-face*, or rather facial transformation, seems surprising, incom-

27

prehensible, almost incredible — it may be a mere
manœuvre to gain time, an easy makeshift of a
man who as readily concludes treaties as he re-
pudiates obligations; or it may just be part of an
improvising political incoherence. Anyhow, it does
not follow the line of Prussia's traditional policy.

But there are people who try to read sense and
a deeper meaning into all actions of rulers. They
reason: Germany cannot renounce the Corridor
and Upper Silesia; she is rearming on a vast scale;
she proclaims her hostility to Russia and her
friendship for Poland; Pilsudski and his group
aimed at one time at further extensive conquests
at the expense of Russia — is perhaps Germany
out to obtain a revision of her eastern frontier in
agreement and co-operation with the Poles, com-
pensating them in the Ukraine, White Russia, and
Lithuania for cessions in the West?

Is such a policy practicable? In the Corridor,
even in 1919, the Poles were in a majority; now
they form 90 per cent of the population. The
Corridor secures Poland's access to the sea; its
retrocession would give Germany an economic
stranglehold on Poland. In Upper Silesia the districts ceded to Poland fall short of what the Poles
can claim on grounds of language and nationality.
All the territory which Germany can possibly
demand from the Poles is ethnically Polish. But
can any nation exchange land inhabited by its own

people against ethnically foreign country? At no price and against no compensation will any Polish Government, of its own free will, agree to such a deal. Would England accept the medieval French Empire of Henry V in compensation for Cornwall or Kent, or France give up Alsace-Lorraine in exchange for Piedmont or Catalonia? Why, then, expect such a thing from the Poles? When Jules Ferry engaged in colonial expansion, not as a compensation for a voluntary cession but as a kind of consolation after the loss of Alsace-Lorraine, Deroulède exclaimed in the Chamber: " I mourn two children and you offer me twenty domestics! "

In the East, provinces inhabited by millions of White Russians and Ukrainians are included within the present frontiers of Poland — an " irredenta " which threatens her existence. Would it be sound policy for the Poles to add to their numbers? This would merely hasten the loss of the non-Polish territories which they now hold. Nor would the creation of satellite States in the Ukraine and White Russia against the Soviets, if at all feasible, work in favour of the Poles. The Moscow Bolsheviks may disinterest themselves in the fate of Ukrainian or White Russian territories under Polish rule; but nationalist States in the Ukraine or White Russia could never evince such indifference. They would become Ger-

many's clients and allies against a Poland sand-
wiched between them. Lastly, the Poles would
never allow German armies to cross their country,
even in order to fight Russia, for they could
hardly trust these armies, once they had entered
the late Prussian provinces, voluntarily to leave
them again.

Hopes or fears of a joint German-Polish expedition against Russia are mere bubbles. If the
Germans hint at such schemes, it may be in order
to cover up Hitler's betrayal of Prussia, or his
manœuvre, or blunder; if the Russians take them
seriously, it is because, having for almost twenty
years cut themselves off from the intercourse of
men, they see ghosts. What then is the purpose
of Germany's armaments? What is the future
direction of her policy, and where is her much
heralded " rehabilitation " to take place? Clearly
armaments and drill for their own sake will not
satisfy a nation indefinitely; nor will the cancel-
ling of some by now meaningless paragraphs of
the Treaty of Versailles justify the effort and
sacrifice implied in rearmament. What Hitler
says or what Hitler thinks matters little. He will
say and he will think different things on different
days, sincerely, with half-sincerity, or without any.
What matters is the direction in which his own
sentimental antecedents and the logic of the situation lead or force him.

There are three Germanies: Western Germany on the Rhine, the Germany of the great Northern plain dominated by Prussia, and Southern, Danubian Germany converging on Austria. Western Germany has almost throughout history been on the defensive, while Berlin and Vienna have been outposts and centres of German expansion. The Prussian lines of advance run along the Baltic and up the Oder and Vistula; the Austrian, towards the Adriatic and into the Balkans. They are historically distinct, divergent, almost contradictory, for they presuppose different policies and alliances. Hindenburg and Ludendorff were Prussians, born in the Eastern provinces, with the cause of the *Ostmarken* in the blood; neither could have renounced the Prussian claims against Poland, and the Junker leaders of the Reichswehr favoured co-operation with Russia, even with Bolshevik Russia, against the Poles. Hitler is an Austrian by birth; the Austrian Germans were nowhere in conflict with the Austrian Poles, and in fact co-operated with them. The main fear and hatred in pre-war Vienna was of Russia, the enemy of the Habsburg Monarchy and of the Poles, and the protector of the Czechs, Yugo-Slavs, and Rumanians. Hitler's readiness to make friends with the Poles and to inveigh against Russia is perhaps an unconscious inheritance from his Austrian past; anyhow, it

31

follows the line of Austria's traditional policy.
Moreover, a crusade against the Bolsheviks would
seem a fitting sequel to his previous domestic
brawls, slogans, and exploits; and by proclaiming
it he hopes to gain the sympathy of the anti-
Bolsheviks abroad, especially in this country, and
to justify in their eyes the rearmament of Germany. But there is no substance behind such talk.
He must know that joint action with the Poles
against Russia is not practical politics.

What, then, is .the present meaning of the
German-Polish agreement (for the meaning of
agreements may vary from time to time)? Hitler
can never renounce Austria, any more than Poincaré could have renounced Lorraine or Pilsudski
Vilna. This is where his past leads him; but
while he engages in a campaign against Austria,
the agreement with the Poles covers his northern
front, both against Poland and against Russia.
To the Poles, on the other hand, who had to fear
that they would become the first object of attack
by a rearmed Germany (backed perhaps by
Russia), the agreement with Germany offers the
assurance that her first attempt to break through
will be on the Danube, and not on the Vistula.

Austria is German, and seemingly the most
plausible claim which Germany can raise for a
revision of the Peace Treaties is that she should be
allowed that measure of national reunion which

was postulated for all other nations at the end of the war. Before the advent of the Nazis, union with Germany was the common programme of all Austrian parties. Now a democratic alliance of Catholics and Socialists in Austria could alone form a bulwark against the Nazi advance or aggression, and was therefore desired by the wisest leaders in both camps. The situation has, however, been messed up by the puppets of Mussolini, who played his own game independently of, or even against, the Little Entente and France. He favoured Hungary and Bulgaria, which, as soon as Germany disclosed her armed strength, declared for her; and he has raised up a nondescript Fascism in Austria which has laid the country open to Nazi intrigues, propaganda, and coups.

Vienna is the focal point on the Danube, and perhaps the most important strategic position in the politics of Central and Eastern Europe. The moment the Nazis successfully set up their standard in Vienna the whole of Central and South-Eastern Europe, from the Bohemian Mountains and the Carpathians down to the Adriatic, Greece, and the Straits, would be aflame, and the political balance of Europe would be destroyed. Czecho-Slovakia, surrounded by Nazis and Magyars, with millions of Nazis within her own borders, would either have to pass into the German orbit or cease to exist; while Yugo-Slavia and Rumania would be attacked from two sides, by the Magyars and the Bulgars. Italy, so far from being able to play a preponderant part in the territories of the old Habsburg Monarchy and in the Balkans, would have to think of her own safety. If then the Western Powers remained passive spectators, German hegemony on the Continent would be re-established, beyond anything known in 1914, more ruthless and more menacing, more brutal and more barbaric.

To sum up: Hitler cannot fight Russia, and could gain nothing by doing so; territorial re-arrangements with Poland are moonshine; while the German-Polish Treaty deflects his activities in the direction in which his own feelings lead him. The Austrian problem has been in the forefront ever since he assumed office. There it remains. Even for reasons of internal German politics, he cannot leave any solidly German territory outside the framework of the " totalitarian State." Agreements can be concluded about Austria and quasi-solutions can be found, without in any way safeguarding the position. For in Austria Hitler can adopt various methods, plausible in appearance and difficult to counter or to dispute. But the enormous armaments, the universal drilling and spiritual militarization of the German people, the tension which has been worked up by him in Germany — all this cannot unload itself in the mere expunging of the " war-guilt lie " or in a theoretical declaration that Germany is fit to hold African colonies. Berchtesgaden is now the emotional centre of an incalculable German policy, and the storm which is brewing threatens Vienna. When it breaks it will not be a merely local disturbance.

FRENCH POLICY IN EUROPE,
1919–1938

(" *Manchester Guardian,*" *October* 22, 1938)

In 1914 there were five Great Powers on the
European Continent, in 1919 only one. Russia
had collapsed, Germany had been defeated, the
Habsburg Monarchy had disappeared, and Italy
had been proved once more no Great Power. In
this void France attained a preponderance seemingly more complete than she had known since
the days of Napoleon I. But in 1815 she still had
a population larger than that of Austria, twice
that of Great Britain, and almost three times that
of Prussia; now she has the smallest population
among the Great Powers. The victory of 1918
was won through the intervention of the Anglo-
Saxon Powers; it produced Poland and the Succession States. France had the choice of seeking
security in political retirement under the wings of
the Anglo-Saxon Powers or of trying to remedy
the disparity in numbers through alliances with
the new States. In victory the temptation to be
once more *une puissance protectrice* proved irresistible — she constructed a system based on satellite

36

nations. France, Poland, and the Little Entente were sufficient to hold in check the three defeated enemies Germany, Hungary, and Bulgaria; it was the essence of the system and its weakness that it contained only one Great Power. A despoiled Russia and an ever-hungry Italy were left outside, antagonized; of uncertain value as military Powers, they count through territory and numbers: dangerous potential allies of Germany.

Poland was the pivot of the French system, the Little Entente its complement. Sentiment and interest seemed to bind Poland to France. Culturally and politically Poland had gravitated towards her, while all France had for over a century been pro-Polish — her Left because the Poles were victims of oppression and alleged champions of liberty, her Right because they were devout Roman Catholics. In 1919, through British action, Poland received less than her due in Danzig and Upper Silesia; yet it was enough to earn her the bitter resentment of Germany. If a reconciliation between France and Germany had been possible, the German-Polish conflict would have sufficed to prevent it. In 1919–20, with French connivance, Poland annexed extensive territories inhabited by White Russians and Ukrainians; it was henceforth a vital interest of Poland that Russia no less than Germany should remain an outcast among the nations. The result was the

German-Russian Treaty concluded at Rapallo in
1922.

Italy always tries, and usually succeeds, by
acquisitions to compensate for the absence of
achievement. She received more than her due at
the expense of Yugo-Slavs, Germans, and Greeks,
and yet felt aggrieved. " She has such poor teeth
and such a large appetite," Bismarck had said
about her. She started to play off Hungary and
Bulgaria against the Little Entente, and to con-
struct a system rival to that of France. On one
point, however, she agreed with France and the
Little Entente: there was to be no *Anschluss* of
Austria to Germany, no German penetration of
the Danube Basin, no German soldiers on the
Brenner Pass. Otherwise Italy came to rank as a
" revisionist " Power.

France by her system had tried to redress her
inferiority in numbers as against Germany; with
Russia and Italy estranged, this disparity threatened
to become even worse. The French Army was
still supreme; none the less France was afraid;
for she did not want to fight again. There was
no real militarism in France, no aggressiveness,
no lust for power, only the wish to be secure. Her
system was proving a liability; she therefore
sought to make Britain share its burden. Our
guarantee for all European frontiers was to be
obtained at Geneva, through pacts and protocols.

Since the war whoever wants to cajole Britain talks peace. But all that France obtained was the Locarno Treaty; no British guarantee for Poland. This was obtained from the Czechs, who within their own frontiers, drawn by nature and history, tried to conciliate the German minority (from 1926 to 1938 there were German Ministers in every Czecho-Slovak Cabinet), and who, if left to themselves, might perhaps have succeeded. The two standing conflicts on the Continent were between Germany and Poland and between Italy and Yugo-Slavia.

The rise of an aggressive German militarism showed up still more clearly the insufficiency of the French system and the French unwillingness to fight. France now accepted Britain's leadership and joined in talks for a Four-Powers Pact. At that stage Germany and Italy would have had to be satisfied at the expense of Poland and Yugo-Slavia; France did not mean to sacrifice her smaller allies, yet made them sore and suspicious. Why should they not in turn enter into direct negotiations with their hitherto hostile neighbours? The juncture was favourable to the Poles: Hitler was not a Prussian but an Austrian, and his first aim was not the recovery of the lost Prussian provinces but the *Anschluss*. Moreover, both at home and abroad he was talking anti-Bolshevism. The Russians became scared, entered the

39

League, and drew closer to France: one more reason for the Poles to work with Hitler. On his part this was a promise not to make them his first object of attack; on theirs, not to interfere with his operations elsewhere; neither seriously envisaged action against Russia.

The Nazi attempt in Vienna in July 1934 alarmed Italy; by the " Stresa Front " the Western Powers assured her of their support. But to the Yugo-Slavs the line Milan–Vienna–Budapest would have been as unwelcome as Munich–Vienna–Budapest to the Czechs. Most of all, Yugo-Slavia objected to a Habsburg restoration because of the attraction it would have had for the discontented Roman Catholic Croats; and such a restoration came to be canvassed as the means for preserving Austria's separate existence. The Yugo-Slavs drew closer to Germany. France was losing two satellites, but seemed to be gaining the co-operation of two Great Powers; exchanging pre-eminence for security.

When Mussolini invaded Abyssinia, and England, in her disarmed condition, half-heartedly tried to fulfil the League Covenant, France struggled to reconcile complaisance towards Italy with Geneva righteousness. The Western Powers neither satisfied nor checked Italy, and lost themselves in half-measures. Sated and sophisticated, civilized, sensitive, and war-weary, the demo-

cracies have a conscience and no faith — the most
dangerous condition for individuals and nations;
and they encounter dictators, savage " revivalists "
without a conscience or sensibility. Political pro-
clivities clash with international alignments: Germany is the ever-menacing enemy of France;
Italy has become hostile to England; Russia has
been turning into an ally. Yet large sections of
opinion both in Britain and in France are pro-
Italian, or even pro-German, and intensely anti-
Russian. This confusion and debility of purpose
has produced the antics of the " non-intervention "
policy in Spain, and has paralysed rearmament.

In 1936 Germany by remilitarizing the Rhine-
land started a barrier against French intervention
in Central and Eastern Europe — additional
justification for the Polish and Yugo-Slav Governments to pursue their new policy, unpopular
though it was with their people. Stalin started his
" purges," which produced dismay among Russia's
friends and raised doubts about her future military value — additional justification for those
averse to a Russian alliance. Mussolini added
Spanish entanglements to his Abyssinian commitments and launched a vicious anti-British campaign
in the Near East. Meantime the armaments and
policy of the Western Powers continued to display
as much of " gaps " as of substance. When Hitler
invaded Austria there was no one to resist him.

He is single-minded and ready to take risks, which makes him supreme over those who do not know their minds and cannot control their fears.

Could the French system have survived the Nazi occupation of Vienna? The Czechs still adhered to it. But they asked the Western Powers: " Do you want us? If not, tell us so, and we shall have to make our terms with Hitler." They never received an honest answer. Had Poland and Yugo-Slavia stood by France, Germany could not have attacked Czecho-Slovakia; had the Western Powers stood by Czecho-Slovakia, Polish and Yugo-Slav public opinion would in the end have compelled the Governments to join them; had Czecho-Slovakia stood fast, she could have forced France into action. For everyone war was fraught with incalculable risks: therefore no one wanted it; but the bluff of the democracies has been called; that of the dictators has not. Now it is all over. The French system has collapsed with unspeakable ignominy. What next?

East-Central Europe will become a witches' cauldron. Poland, Yugo-Slavia, and Rumania are as composite as Czecho-Slovakia had been; all their " Sudetens " are agog — there is scope for housebreakers. The security of the French system was collective: last month its quondam members dug their own graves. And if Russia is ever added to the German system — by agreement with the Bolsheviks or by their overthrow — a Power will arise greater than the world has known.

France has 40 million inhabitants, Germany 80 millions, Italy 40 millions; to which Spain, when handed over to Franco, will add 20 millions: a superiority of 100 millions for the " axis." Can Britain alone ensure the integrity and independence of France, and therefore her own? It is idle to expect a victorious totalitarian and his jackals to be satisfied with reasonable concessions.

The key to the situation is in the relations of the British Empire and France to the United States and Russia.

THE POLISH CORRIDOR AND UPPER SILESIA

("*Manchester Guardian,*" *November* 7, 1933)

THE problem of the Polish Corridor is not one of right against wrong; it results from a conflict of two principles, of the unity of the seaboard *versus* the unity of the river-basin. Which of the two should prevail? In the Middle Ages the Germans advanced quickly along the Baltic coast, with the sea for their base, and established themselves at Riga not much later than at Berlin. The Poles, on the other hand, are the nation of the Vistula, and their settlements extend from the sources of the river to its estuary; there is no other European nation centred to that extent on one single river. It is only fair that the claim of the river-basin should prevail against that of the seaboard. The Baltic joins East Prussia to Pomerania, even while the Polish Corridor intervenes between them; whereas without access to the sea Poland would be deprived of her main and most natural connexion with the outer world and of the freedom which is secured by it. The cutting through of the Corridor has meant a

44

minor amputation for Germany; its closing up would mean strangulation for Poland.

Within the Corridor the Germans formed, according to their own census of 1910, less than half of the population; thus even numerically they had no superior claim to that territory. By 1921, according to the Polish census, the proportion of Germans had sunk to less than 21, and by December, 1931, to only 10 per cent. Some Germans undoubtedly left because they would not live under the dominion of a race which they had previously oppressed and despised; others are said to have been squeezed out by the Poles. Even if this is so, the question must be asked how many of those Germans had originally been planted artificially in that country by the Prussian Government, or why their attachment to it proved so weak and their courage and staying power so faint? No Germans in that territory were treated by the Poles with the barbarity with which tens of thousands of German citizens are now treated in Germany for reasons of race or of political opinions.

As for Upper Silesia, it is alleged on reliable authority that severe and unfair pressure, in a sense hostile to the Germans, was exercised there before and during the plebiscite, and that the frontier drawn by the League of Nations, on the supposed basis of the plebiscite, is not fair to the

Germans. But if the peace settlement is to be questioned and revised, let this be done thoroughly; and my contention is that there ought never to have been a plebiscite in Upper Silesia, but that the frontier should have been drawn on the linguistic basis. Had that been done, the Poles would have obtained far more territory than they have by all the manœuvres carried out in connexion with the plebiscite.

A plebiscite is a tolerably efficient method for settling frontiers only where the national consciousness of the inhabitants is fully crystallized. In Slesvig everyone knew whether he was a German or a Dane, and the same would have held good as between, say, the Turks and the Greeks; but it was not true in Upper Silesia. In 1871, in an appeal to the Germans not to annex Alsace-Lorraine, the Polish-speaking inhabitants of Upper Silesia were quoted as example of a population whose national consciousness would never again coincide with their language; but some thirty years later the first Polish Nationalist was returned from Upper Silesia to the German Reichstag, and by 1914 there were several. At the time of the plebiscite two-thirds of the population in the area in which it was taken spoke Polish, and one-third German; but only one half of the Polish-speaking population voted for Poland. The Polish national revival in

Upper Silesia was progressing steadily, but was still far from having reached its natural term in 1919. There is such a thing as a nationality *in posse* besides a nationality *in esse*, and a plebiscite is not justified in districts which are in a state of change and transition. Whatever injustice may have been committed against Germany in the execution or interpretation of the Silesian plebiscite, the plebiscite itself was an injustice against Poland.

JUDAICA

E

EXPANSION OF AREAS OF ACUTE JEWISH EMIGRATION
NEED OR PERSECUTION

Reproduced from " Palestine and Middle East " (Tel-Aviv), Oct./Nov. 1938

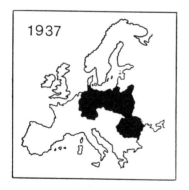

THE PALESTINE VANISHING TRICK

Progressive Reduction in Jewish Settlement Areas

Reproduced from " Palestine and Middle East " (Tel-Aviv)
Oct./Nov. 1938 ; with a postscript for 1939

PALESTINE OF
BALFOUR DECLARATION

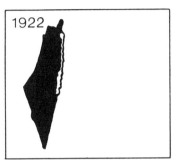

PALESTINE OF THE MANDATE

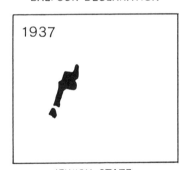

JEWISH STATE
(ROYAL COMMISSION)

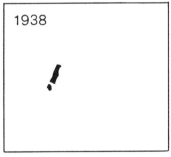

JEWISH STATE
(WOODHEAD COMMISSION)

JEWISH PALESTINE
(MACDONALD WHITE PAPER)

THE JEWS IN THE MODERN
WORLD [1]

A few years before the Nazi revolution a Japanese diplomatist in Berlin asked Dr. Solf, late Ambassador to Tokyo, to recommend to him a Professor of anti-Semitism. Being told that there was no such Chair in the University — " What! " exclaimed the Japanese, " you talk anti-Semitism day and night, and have no one to teach it? " " But anyhow, what do you need it for? " asked Dr. Solf. " You have no Jews." " No, we haven't," was the reply, " but we hear that they are coming, and so we want to be prepared."

Presumably the Japanese diplomatist desired to obtain accurate information concerning a people whom he heard described as dangerous and unpleasant; and we Jews can wish that many anti-Semites, or potential anti-Semites, should share his desire. Our position in the world is anomalous, difficult, and often ambiguous; and not everyone who feels uncomfortable with regard to us must be called an anti-Semite, nor is there anything

[1] Published in February 1934 as Introduction to Dr. Ruppin's book, " The Jews in the Modern World."

necessarily and inherently wicked in anti-Semit-ism. Nations do not like each other and they dis-like strangers in their midst; but what others can bear with comparative, or even cheerful, indiffer-ence is made painful for us by our defenceless, helpless condition, and by the fact that we Jews frequently do not feel " strangers " where we are looked upon as such. Still, we have a right to demand from anti-Semites, if sane and civilized, that they should honestly try to acquaint them-selves with the facts of the problem which seems to exercise their minds, and that in forming their conclusions they should show a measure of good sense and common kindness without which no difficult problem can be successfully tackled.

Even more do we require such information to guide our own counsels and actions. For what-ever the non-Jewish world may or may not do to us, and however much we may depend on it, ultimately our fate is in our hands; our interest in our own future is such that if focussed and rightly directed, it must prove decisive. The issue of a crisis depends not so much on its magnitude as on the courage and resolution with which the crisis is met.

Numbers affect our problem in a peculiar manner: to a nation rooted in its own soil, com-plete in its social structure, and therefore reasonably self-sufficient, they mean strength and security, but for us, outside Palestine, they have always constituted a danger. This was, and is, the curse of the *Galuth* (the Exile); a nation cannot, and must not, grow except in soil which it can call its own. Even where we form one-tenth of the population, we are helpless against a hostile attack by the organized forces of the majority. We cannot sustain an economic attack, for our occupational structure lacks inner balance; and we are morally unarmed for a political struggle, even where we have a strong communal or national consciousness. Attachment to home and country give a man the strength to fight; but such love, in the *Galuth*, binds us through the land to the community and State which are built upon it, that means to the " majority-nation "; though this does not necessarily bind them to us. Faced by Nazi persecutions, many Jews who had felt German and had fought and worked for Germany, committed suicide from humiliation and despair; such suicides were greeted with glee by the Nazi press, which voiced the hope that many more Jews would take leave of Germany in that way.

As a rule, we are safest where we are few — where we receive individual treatment, fit ourselves into the national framework, and can rise without arousing attention or jealousy. In such circumstances we most quickly dissolve and disappear,

53

and reach that supreme security which for the Jews in the Diaspora lies in non-existence. This was the path of certain old European Jewries, and would, within measurable time, have been that of German Jewry, if they had had to deal with a normal people. Still, for the main body of the Jewish people the nineteenth century (which extends till 1914) was not an age of numerical decline, but of the greatest expansion.

At the destruction of the Jewish State, in 70 A.D., our numbers are estimated to have been $4\frac{1}{2}$ millions, of whom, even then, only a million inhabited Palestine; the greatest part were scattered from Baghdad to Alexandria. This was the Oriental period of Jewish history.

In the eleventh century the spiritual and political centre of world-Jewry began to shift to Spain, and by 1492 the Sephardic Jews formed, even numerically, the most important body in Jewry. With the persecutions and expulsions which set in about that time, closes the Spanish, or Iberian, period of our history.

During the next three centuries, our numbers remained low, and when, by 1800, world-Jewry reached the figure of about $2\frac{1}{2}$ millions, nearly half of it inhabited the territories of the late Kingdom of Poland. This shifting of the centre was probably due at least as much to differences in the rate of natural increase as to migrations — before the end of the eighteenth century, towns were the graveyards of population, and in Poland alone did the Jews live largely in rural, or semi-rural, surroundings. The nineteenth century is in our history the period of the numerical preponderance of the Yiddish-speaking Jew of Eastern Europe, and of the intellectual and economic predominance of the German Jew.

The outstanding feature of the period 1750–1914 was the rapid growth of European populations, based on a reduction of the death-rate, especially the infantile death-rate; it started in the West, spread eastward, and was followed, and ultimately counterbalanced, by a fall in the birth-rate. Possibly the complex of phenomena described as " progress," which, at one time, seemed to us a law of nature and history, was basically connected with the rapid growth of population. This called for expansion and change, for thought, research, and freedom; and these principles, being dominant, were carried, by a curious process of percolation common in the history of human thought, into every province of life. At the same time there occurred an enormous growth of cities; mass-migrations overseas; a widening of the " political nation "; a strong increase in the numbers of the professional intelligentsia and black-coated workers — all this against the background of the capitalist system, based at first on freedom of trade and competition, but hardening subsequently into nationalized or trustified organizations.

Two races headed the movement, though under vastly different conditions — the British and the Jews; they were the pioneers of capitalism, and its first, and perhaps chief, beneficiaries. They were the first to reduce their death-rate, and to achieve a great natural increase; a greater proportion from among them emigrated than from any other nation; they are now the two most urban communities; and the two most widely scattered in the world; have the largest percentage of black-coated workers and professional intelligentsia; and are threatened by the rise of the corresponding classes in countries in which they live dispersed. They have worked for other nations, not for profit only, but with an idealism for which they are seldom given credit, and have rendered services — the Jews among the white races and the British in dark continents — for which they are not thanked; and they have both preached ideas of world-wide freedom and world-wide co-operation, on which the others have turned their backs. Now both have to face the problem of restoring their own inner economic balance, and of achieving a measure of self-sufficiency.

But the Englishman can say: " We are a world Power; our retreat within our Empire is largely governed by our own will and choice; we can regulate its pace; there is force in us if we choose to employ it; and we can fall back upon this island which we have neglected while developing continents; we can, and shall, develop it; we have the resources of a State with which to re-establish the balance of our economy and a necessary measure of economic independence; if need be, we have the means for an intense and successful economic and political nationalism."

The Jew, on the other hand, must say: " In the Galuth we are like so many slaves and hostages dependent on the will of others; we may be well treated, or badly; if badly, we have hardly the means for self-defence; if we have to retreat, the pace of our retreat is prescribed by others; we must now undergo a fundamental process of economic re-orientation, but we have neither the resources of a State nor the place wherein to effect it; all our strength is in a faith mixed with despair, and all the space we can claim is Palestine, our Promised Land, now the ' half-promised ' land of Mandatory politics; moreover we have grown so numerous that Palestine can hold but a fraction of our people, and so poor that it is only with the greatest difficulty that we can raise the means for developing even the limited possibilities of Palestine."

Here is the last century of Jewish history in

figures: in 1825 there were $3\frac{1}{4}$ million Jews; 1850, $4\frac{3}{4}$; 1880, $7\frac{1}{2}$; 1900, $10\frac{1}{2}$; 1925, 15; 1933, nearly 16 millions.

In 1825, $2\frac{1}{4}$ million Jews inhabited Eastern Europe, while the remaining million was almost equally divided between the other European and the Oriental Jews; only about 10,000 lived in America.

Oriental Jewry, even in the nineteenth century, continued to inhabit medieval ghettoes; their increase was small, and their proportion in world-Jewry dropped from 16·5 per cent in 1825 to something over 7 per cent in 1900.

The Jews of Western and Central Europe had a considerable natural increase till about 1850, and a slow increase during the next 30-50 years; but owing to a very low birth-rate in more recent times, and to considerable losses through mixed marriages and baptisms, they would probably by now have been reduced to the figure of 1850, had it not been for immigration from Eastern Europe. It was there that the main increase occurred.

Of the $7\frac{1}{2}$ million Jews in 1880, almost three-fourths inhabited Eastern Europe, or rather the great Yiddish-speaking Pale which stretched from Riga to Odessa, and from Cracow to Vilna and Kiev. Between 1800 and 1880, that Pale had extended slightly along its eastern and southern edges, in White Russia and the Ukraine, and into

THE JEWS IN THE MODERN WORLD

Kherson, Bessarabia, Moldavia, and, across the Carpathians, into Hungary; while its western fringes, in Prussian Poland, had melted away, through migrations to Central and Western Germany, to England and America. But in the main the Jewry of the Pale remained solid, unmoved, unchanged.

In 1882 started the Jewish mass-migrations, mainly to America; and fifty years later, less than half of world-Jewry was left in Eastern Europe. While in 1825 only three Jews in a thousand inhabited America, and in 1880 three in a hundred, now the proportion is roughly three in ten; but owing to the strong natural increase of those years, the present Jewish population of the East European Pale still exceeds, in absolute figures, that of 1880, and is at least equal to that of 1900.

About 1830 the Jewish birth-rate in Prussia was 35 per thousand, and in Eastern Europe it continued at this, or even at a higher, figure till near the end of the century. But by 1930 the Jewish birth-rate in Vienna was only about 6 per thousand, in Prussia about 9, in Hungary 11, in Rumania 16, and in Poland 20 per thousand. Had the drop in the birth-rate occurred in Eastern Europe some fifty years ago, or had the death-rate remained at its previous level a century longer, there would probably be now no serious Jewish problem in the world. It is the rapid growth in the nineteenth century which is responsible for our present situation; a nation living under desperately anomalous conditions finds sorrow in that which to others would mean a gain.

Politically and economically the nineteenth century, and especially its second half, was the age of the preponderance of the Germans on the European Continent, and of the German Jews in world-Jewry; but the Germans did not know, nor cared to know, for how much of their economic and intellectual primacy they were indebted to the Jews. In 1914 the Jews of Germany and Western Austria were (in proportion to their numbers) the richest, best educated, and most highly cultured Jewish community in the world. While the Jewish proletariat from the East European Pale migrated mainly to the United States, Great Britain, and the British Dominions — i.e. to the English-speaking countries — the intelligentsia and upper middle class were tending towards German Central Europe; the Pale, which at that time had neither a nationality nor a capital of its own, became a kind of Jewish *hinterland* to Central Europe. It was thus that the age of the great numerical preponderance of the East European Jew became that of the economic and cultural predominance of the German Jew.

In about four-fifths of the Pale, Russian was

60

the official language, without being in most parts even the language of its non-Jewish population; while Russia's capitals, St. Petersburg and Moscow, were distant and practically closed to the Jews — and so were its schools and Universities, under the *numerus clausus*. From Yiddish there was an easy transition to German, and the Austrian and German High Schools and Universities were nearest to the Pale and open to the East European Jews. To the Jews of Galicia, of the Czech provinces, and to some extent even of Hungary, Vienna was the social and intellectual capital, and for a certain number a station on the road to Berlin; while Berlin and other German towns became intellectual and economic centres for the Russian, Polish, and Rumanian Jews. Tens of thousands received their training in Germany; most of them subsequently returned to their homes and involuntarily served there as channels for German intellectual and economic penetration — which did not make the Jews more popular in the countries concerned. Again, in English-speaking countries the German Jews, especially those of Frankfort and Hamburg, served as intermediaries and interpreters for the Germans, who themselves hardly excel in dealings with other nations. Men like Sir Ernest Cassel or Mr. Jacob Schiff, to mention two outstanding examples, while loyal to the countries of their adoption, preserved a regard and attachment for the country of their origin; and again the Jews as a whole suffered from the supposed German taint. The only people who never recognized, or perhaps never realized, the services rendered by the Jews to Germany, were the Germans themselves. They believed the Jews to be powerful; they knew, or ought to have known, that the German Jews were devoted to Germany; they might have known what, under these conditions, was the value of having the economic and intellectual centre of world-Jewry within their borders. But the pleasure derived from insulting and humiliating other men outweighed every consideration — this being the way in which some people establish, or restore, their self-appreciation.

Moreover the Jew is fundamentally uncongenial to the German. The German is methodical, crude, constructive mainly in a mechanical sense, extremely submissive to authority, a rebel or a fighter only by order from above; he gladly remains all his life a tiny cog in a machine. The Leviathan State of modern German political theory and practice is a psychological counterpart to Germany's previous division into hundreds of petty States, and both are the expression of German political and social ineptitude. The Jew, of Oriental or Mediterranean race, is creative, pliable, individualistic, restless, and undisciplined; he could have formed a useful complement and corrective to the German. But the German could not digest him — as Nietzsche says: " German intellect is indigestion; it can assimilate nothing." German culture is perhaps the least national of all cultures; it is essentially middle-class and urban in origin, the landed classes in Germany (in contradistinction to England and France, Poland and Hungary) having contributed little to it; it started in abstract thought, and finished in crude materialism. It is perhaps because German culture is urban that the Jews found it easiest to work in it. And perhaps Caliban's ill-humour, and next his fury, are due to — but it is not worth speculating here about their reasons.

In the terms of the German culture the Jews did great work, for which the Germans received the credit, giving none in turn to the Jews. It was only after the Nazi revolution had driven out Einstein, Reinhardt, and Bruno Walter that the world at large realized they were Jews. The same could be said of hundreds of other men. But there is no need to argue the point. The contention of the Nazis is not that the Jews were unimportant or ineffective, but that they held too many leading positions, and that their work was " unwholesome " for the " Aryan " Germans. Of what is " wholesome " for these, they alone must be the judges; but as for the number of leading positions held by Jews, especially in the liberal professions, no one who has known Germany even in pre-Nazi days will believe that Jews had obtained them on the strength of being Jews. Legal exclusion and the concentration camp are now used, where no handicap, however severe, had proved sufficient.

The war, which destroyed the political and economic predominance of Germany and Austria-Hungary, went far to shatter that of their Jews in world-Jewry. Russia cut herself off from the outer world; the Border and Succession States, strongly nationalist and in most cases anti-German, cut themselves off from Central Europe; German and German-Jewish influence was waning. Inflation destroyed a great part of the wealth of Central European Jewry; their trade was shrinking. The financial centre of world-Jewry had moved to New York, and the political centre, because of the Palestine Mandate, to London; and with nearly one-third of world-Jewry removed to English-speaking countries, its centre of gravity was anyhow bound to shift. The change was delayed by the fact that a very large proportion of the Jewish immigrants still lived as workmen and small traders on the East Side of New York, in the East End of London, or in the ghettoes of Canadian and South African cities; the full effect of the migration will only be felt in time — for whatever may be said of us, be it good or bad, no one denies that we count for something.

64

The nineteenth-century connexion with the Germans was a disaster for us. As slaves — even worse, as voluntary captives — the German Jews built an Arch of Titus for Germany, and such was their attachment to the country that, had the Germans merely proceeded slowly, they could have still gone a long way in the moral abasement of the Jews without losing their services. But now the Nazis deliberately and systematically cut the remaining threads of the Jewish net of which Germany had been the centre. All that we Jews can, and should, do in self-respect is to help them to cut these threads.

When the head of Louis XVI fell, all the monarchs of Europe felt their necks; when the blow fell on the head of German Jewry, many of us other Jews began to wonder what the future had in store for various branches of our people. It is too early to pronounce a judgment, but high time to consider our position; and though no other, not even the culturally most backward country, is likely to display the same disregard of human rights — at least not without producing a reaction among its own people — there is no doubt that in one way or another the German example will stimulate anti-Semitic movements in other countries. We must not overrate the significance of the German catastrophe, but we must not

65   F

underrate it either. We must look at the facts and consider fundamentals.

This, approximately, was the picture of the Jewish fate and future as it appeared to many of us a few years ago:

The time of the great Jewish migrations had come to an end. A disillusioned, morally unsettled, and economically impoverished world was freezing in once more, after the great movements of a now defunct age. It seemed that intercommunications in world-Jewry would diminish, though the common work of building up the National Home in Palestine would still hold us together for a while, at least the keenest among us; and there, in the Land of Israel, the branch would survive about which Isaiah prophesied, perhaps a branch sounder than any, since our national tree was uprooted from its native soil. The Jews of Western and Central Europe would die out or dwindle into insignificance, and many of us thought that this process, though diversified by vituperation and occasional outbreaks on the part of the coarser among our " hosts," would on the whole take an increasingly peaceful character. The only Jewries which seemed to matter were the $4\frac{1}{2}$ millions in the United States, the 3 millions in Poland, an almost equal number in Soviet Russia, and nearly one million in Roumania.

The future of the American Jews was, and

remains, to most of us, a closed book, like that of America herself. Even though their natural increase is high at present — the younger age-groups among them are still always dispropor-tionately large — they will, within measurable time, become numerically stationary. Culturally, for good and for bad, they will soon have shed every vestige of their East European extraction. What will then replace their fading, anaemic Judaism? How deep and how far will assimilation and amalgamation proceed? Or will they be kept together by anti-Semitic pressure, after their own inner values have disappeared? If so, on what will they live, culturally and morally? Will they at least maintain themselves economically? They now form numerically the largest, and financially (even after the crash of 1929–33) the most im-portant unit in world-Jewry.

The war and revolutions have wrought the economic ruin of the East European Jews, and it was the unstinted help of American Jewry which alone secured the survival of many hundreds of thousands among them. But that support cannot, and will not, be continued indefinitely, and private help naturally diminishes as the ties which bound the emigrants of 1882–1914 to relatives in their old homes weaken with every death on either side of the Atlantic.

In Soviet Russia Jewry faces dissolution.

Religion and occupational segregation acted in the Diaspora as barriers to social intercourse, assimilation, and intermarriage. But in Russia the Jewish religion is dying, and the Jewish professions have been destroyed. Herded together in the Pale of Settlement, the Jews were bound to remain a distinct community, for no one can be assimilated to a nation in the abstract, and there were no types within their sphere to which they could have been assimilated. They are now moving out from the Pale, and everywhere tend to engage in the same work as the rest of the population, which is a healthy development, but, if continued for a few generations, may lead to the extinction of Russian Jewry. That economic reorientation which still awaits us in many a country, and which in Palestine our pioneers have voluntarily taken upon themselves for the sake of the national idea, has been effected in Bolshevik Russia with a suddenness and ruthlessness peculiar to that régime, but also with a certain humanity for which credit is due to it: the Bolsheviks at least feel an obligation to provide manual work for the Jews who apply for it, and do not consider that Jews, because they are Jews, should be deprived of their livelihood without being given a chance of finding another. That the attempts to provide such chances have often been extremely ineffectual, and that very large numbers of Jews in Soviet Russia have perished

68

of misery and privations, is part of the gruesome post-war history of the Jews and of Russia.

In other East European countries the same is happening in a slower, but no less deadly, manner. The Jewish petty traders and artisans are being ruined by factories, large stores, co-operatives, etc., and individual Jewish enterprise by the economic activities of the State and of big syndicates; and all along such national organizations cut out the Jews from employment. The burden of unemployment is, by preference, thrown upon them, without a dole. The Jewish population is faced by hopeless pauperization. Emigration has stopped, one country after another having closed its gates; and, in absolute figures, the number of Jews in Eastern Europe is still on the increase. What is to become of them?

In 1932 the problem of Polish Jewry, and also of those of Rumania and Lithuania, seemed the most burning problem; and when the impact of the Nazi outburst has passed, it will probably once more appear to us in that light. But shall we still see it with the same eyes as in 1932? At that time it seemed to us that our foremost endeavour should be directed towards fighting the " *Luft-mensch* " — this untranslatable term describes men without solid ground under their feet, without training or profession, without capital or regular employment, living in the air, and, it would

69

almost seem, on air. For a long time past, their
number has been appallingly high in the over-
crowded ghettoes of Eastern Europe, and in 1932
we thought that our first task was to change that
type of man into a sound earner. But the German
experience of 1933 has taught us that a Jew
occupying a foremost place in his profession may,
overnight, be turned into a *Luftmensch*, by being
forbidden to exercise it in the land of his birth,
and not allowed to take it up in any other country.
Greater than the tragedy of individual Jewish un-
employables in Eastern Europe is the *Luftmensch*
tragedy of us all, due to the fact that as a nation
we have no firm ground under our feet; man
cannot live outside a community, but he is truly
safe in his own community only — it has to be
his own, in the fullest, completest sense. In fact,
even the unsound economic character of individual
Jews in the past merely reflected the condition of
the nation. It was its anomalous position which
had made so many of us into traders or into " intellectuals " (another kind of *Luftmenschen*), and had
kept us out of the more solid, enduring occupations; while those who entered such occupations,
especially those who settled as peasants among
peasants, or as squires among squires, soon struck
root and mingled with the growth of the soil.
They ceased to be Jews, and found an individual
solution of the problem. But now at last the

problem has to be solved, one way or another, for our people as a whole.

Among European nations, during the best part of the nineteenth century, the upper and middle classes alone were articulate; they moved and worked free from obsolete shackles and as yet not drawn down by the weight of the masses. Fundamentally they thought of themselves as " the nation," even if this limitation was unconscious; and it was primarily on that comparatively narrow basis that individualism developed. The existence of the mute crowd in the background was politely acknowledged, and then passed over; or it was contended that their problems could be solved in the same terms as those of the upper strata.

The solution of the Jewish problem in the terms of the period was individual assimilation. But this was a feasible programme only so long as applied to small, scattered groups, or merely to the upper classes in large Jewish communities; dense masses, living in a world of their own, cannot be effectively " assimilated." Individual Jews rose to wealth, distinction, and social rank, and in most cases, they, or their descendants, ceased to be Jews (as happens also with Dissenters in England). The great masses of the Jewish people remained poor, ill-adjusted to their surroundings, and even to each other, for they did

71

not form a self-sufficing, and self-protecting economic entity; and they had no one to speak for
them except in terms about as well suited to their
needs, economic and moral, as Smiles's *Self-Help*
was to those of the British working classes.

The rise of Jewish democracy, *i.e.* the entry of
the Jewish masses into politics, was bound to
result in the rise of a Jewish nationalism, unpleasant and disturbing to the " better-class " Jew
who had made his exit from integral Judaism, or
was hesitating in the nameless realms of half-
sincere compromise. He was high-minded, broad-
minded, open-minded, and without roots, for he
lacked the live touch with any living community.
He wanted to become assimilated and yet to remain apart, trying to stop short of what alone
could have fully achieved the ideal of assimilation
— the complete merging of the Jews in the community in which they lived. His conception of
Judaism merely as a religion was curiously superficial and self-contradictory. For that which dis-
tinguishes the Jewish religion in its modern form
from, say, Christian Unitarianism, is merely the
national tradition which most of the adherents of
Liberal or Reform Judaism profess to reject. By
refraining from complete amalgamation and by
maintaining their separate racial and historical
identity, of which they deny the existence, they
have kept themselves suspended in mid-air —

moral *Luftmenschen*, who provoke criticism among their own people and distrust among the non-Jews. In reality, most of them were perfectly sincere within the limits of their own conscious thinking; they did not avow their insincerity even to themselves. But they forgot that no door can for ever remain half-open.

For centuries we have led an anomalous existence, and assimilation to the rest of the world is the only way out of it. Assimilation can, however, bear two opposite, but complementary and equally admissible, interpretations. Assimilation to a community means for individual Jews intermarriage and disappearance (as happened in the case of the Huguenots in England, after they had at first tried to maintain the separate existence of their Church and community); while in terms of Israel as a whole it can mean one thing only — national reintegration. Jewish nationalism expresses the desire of the Jewish people to be like unto all nations, to be neither the chosen race of our own past imaginings, nor the pariahs into which others have persistently tried, and still try, to depress us; but a nation socially and economically complete, with a Mother Country and a Father State of its own, no longer an orphan.

Our chief aim now must be normality. Whether national reintegration is possible also in the Galuth, or only in Palestine, it is too early to say. Die out we may through mixed marriages with non-Jews, or through birth control, and both these tendencies have been on the increase for some time past. But the question which the Jews must now ask themselves is whether they can, and should, assume the responsibility for bringing Jewish children into the world in the Galuth, to face a fate which seems to become worse every year. It is admitted that parents should not have children for whom they cannot provide economically; but is not the moral basis of existence at least equally important?

The first reaction of some Jews to this contention is that we are a valuable element and ought not to die out, even in the Diaspora. Valuable — to whom? And if it is so, who will lose by our dying out? Not we ourselves. There is no loss in non-existence. And the world outside Palestine? Looking back at our history of the last two thousand years we may perhaps be excused for not worrying as to whether that world will lose or gain by our disappearance.

Other Jews will cry out against " surrender " to our enemies. Why pay even so much attention to our enemies? There is no surrender in a determined exit. The people who will miss us most are the anti-Semites; like the Nazis in a small German town who are said to have wired to Hitler to send them some Jews forthwith or the boycott

74

of April 1 [1933] would be a failure. There is an infinitely difficult time before us, and the man who has children must consider their safety and future, and is bound by hostages to the world. Very few Jewish children have been born in Germany since 1933. Should any be born elsewhere in the Galuth? Unless the half-life of those long centuries can be changed at last into an integral national existence, had it not better come to an end? Whatever will there is in us for Jewish survival must now be focused on the common national future.

The oldest inscription which mentions the Jews by name is a monument by an Egyptian Pharaoh who boasts of having exterminated Israel and left none to survive. We have survived, and our existence has become an obsession to innumerable non-Jews and a burden to most of us. During the first seventeen or eighteen centuries of the Christian era there was the hope of the Messianic miracle which made us indifferent to sufferings and persecution, and gave meaning to our survival in the Exile. We waited for the deliverance of His coming, when all the Jews, even the dead buried in the Galuth, were to have followed Him back to Erets Israel. The hope of the Return lives, and is the only hope which has not failed us; but perhaps His work must be done through the labour of men.

75

In the age of " enlightenment " the place of the Messianic creed was taken by a belief in humanity and progress, in democracy and the rights and brotherhood of man. That creed is gone, or at least survives only in some cultured circles in its original homelands in Western Europe. But we cannot wait for the humanization of mankind.

When the middle classes on the Continent turned anti-Semite, some Jews pinned their faith on Socialism. Anti-Semitism was a " bourgeois " prejudice — as if at the rise of the middle classes it had not been decried as a feudal or clerical superstition! But there is no reason why an ultra-nationalist, anti-Semitic Communism should not arise. Capitalism, in its individualist outlook and its original demand for economic freedom, was international; Communism, aiming at a nationalized economy, is basically national, and its internationalism will probably disappear like that of the French Revolution. And then woe to him who in a Socialist community will be considered a stranger! He will be what the *déclassé* is in Bolshevik Russia.

A little philanthropy for our poorest brethren, a good dose of self-deception, Zionism remembered on festive occasions (like the religion of some Jews remembered during the High Holidays), and the burden of the Jewish question once more shifted on to the children with a polite assurance that a better future awaits them — this will not do any longer. We have no right to shift it on to another generation. A solution in our time is required. Those now alive and conscious of the facts of our situation have to solve the age-long problem before they have the right to produce a further generation. Only those Jews who can build up for themselves a life as members of their nation, a nation even as all other nations, have a right to survive as Jews into the time to come.

VIENNA JEWRY

(" *Manchester Guardian*," *April* 4, 1938)

On the eve of the Nazi invasion the Jewish population of Austria amounted to a total of about 180,000, and of these some 167,000, almost 93 per cent, inhabited Vienna. In 1923 the respective figures were 220,208 and 201,513; in 1934: 191,481 and 176,043. Thus in the course of fifteen years the Jewish population of Austria had decreased by 18 per cent, and by 5 per cent in the last four years. In fact, there was a marked acceleration in this process of numerical attrition: in 1937 the number of Jewish births in Vienna had dropped to 720 — that is, 4 per thousand — probably the lowest birth-rate anywhere on record, and the number of deaths during the same year amounted to 2824 — that is, to 17 per thousand. Besides, 620 persons left the community and only 262 joined it. In short, in that one year, not counting emigration, the Jewish population of Vienna decreased by $1\frac{1}{2}$ per cent. It was a dying community.

Everywhere alike the birth-rate among the Jewish upper and middle classes is very low — on the European Continent much lower than among the non-Jews — and Vienna Jewry belongs almost entirely to these classes. Great numbers among them were, even before the advent of the Nazis, in very straitened circumstances. But these people were, most of them, impoverished rather than poor, and the *nouveaux pauvres* have naturally the lowest birth-rate. The disruption of the Habsburg Monarchy, the kronen *déroute*, and the progressive decay of Vienna had destroyed much of their occupations and substance, while the growth of anti-Semitism under Dollfuss and Schuschnigg was still further narrowing the range of employment for their children. In consequence a good many young Jews have left Austria in the last ten or fifteen years. In Germany, after five years of Nazi government, about half of the Jewish population is over fifty years of age, the young having naturally emigrated in much larger numbers. In Vienna, owing to the exceptionally low birth-rate since the war and to economic factors, this stage has probably been reached already. This simplifies, in a way, what might be called the " active solution " of the problem. But the fate of the many lonely, elderly people who can neither hope for successful resettlement abroad nor have anyone to join there will be bitter indeed. A large number among them have for years past lived on the brink of destitution or have been supported by

others who, under the changed conditions, will
not be able to support them any longer. No
wonder that an unparalleled number of suicides
is daily occurring among the Vienna Jews and
non-Aryans.

The number of Jews and non-Aryans is as
difficult to assess in Vienna as in Germany, and
similar exaggerations are committed in estimating
it. Some even maintain that the Jews and non-
Aryan Christians form together about 40 per cent
of Vienna's population — which is an obvious
absurdity. The vast majority of the Jews and
nearly all the traceable non-Aryans belong to the
upper and middle classes, as intermarriages and
baptisms were virtually limited to the educated.
If therefore the Jews and non-Aryan Christians
formed together anything like 40 per cent of the
population, the upper and middle classes, adding
their Aryan members, would have to comprise more
than half the population, which is clearly impossible. The non-Aryan Christians in Vienna may
be, and probably are, about equal in number to
the Jews and, if that is so, these two groups together form the greater part of Vienna's educated
and well-to-do inhabitants, which adds to the
social-revolutionary joys of the Nazi upheaval.
For there would obviously be much less fun in
making people scrub pavements, or wash windows,
whose profession or habit it is to do so every day,

than to set such tasks to men and women of standing and refinement. Nazism, from the very outset as far as the Jews are concerned, starts with the worst characteristics of what is usually described as Bolshevism — disregard of the rights of persons and of property, and the joy of humiliating people of higher standing and education than their tormentors. But, with all that, it still offers to its adepts the comfort of high " nationalist " respectability and orthodoxy. Only for how long can this movement be directed against the Jews alone? This question will arise in Vienna even sooner than in Germany.

Even the statement that the Jews and non-Aryans together form probably the greater part of Vienna's educated or well-to-do classes tells only part of the story. In the Habsburg Monarchy the " Aryan " intelligentsia of the German provinces, and especially of Vienna, filled the upper ranks of the Civil Service and of the Army of a great State, leaving trade and the professions to a high extent to the Jews and non-Aryans. In fact, having for generations continued in the service of the State (and having even in this proved much inferior to the Germans of the " Reich "), the Austrian Germans have contributed disproportionately little to the cultural and economic development of Vienna. The best-known Vienna intellectuals — at least, most of those known abroad — are (or were) Jews: Schnitzler and Werfel among writers, Freud and Adler among psychologists, Friedjung, Redlich, and Pribram among historians, Mahler among musicians, to say nothing of doctors and scientists. With these men and their potential successors the best part of what the world was accustomed to consider Viennese culture will be laid to rest. The Austrian " Aryan " lower middle class has produced Hitler, who most truly represents its spirit — a mixture of the lower middle class anti-Semitism of suburban Vienna with the racial Pan-Germanism of Graz and the Sudetenland. This the Austrians have given to the common German Fatherland (Hitler proudly describes himself as " Austria's historic contribution to the Great German Reich "). It now comes back to them, developed and systematized in Germany, and it will continue in Austria its work of destruction.

Industry and trade in Vienna were to an overwhelming extent in Jewish hands, and among the Aryan industrialists, even in the past, some of the most prominent were Protestant immigrants from the Reich. The Jews will now be systematically squeezed out of their economic positions; but so much seems certain — their places will not be filled by Austrian Aryans but by German brethren from across the frontier, especially as those branches of Austrian trade alone have a chance of developing or surviving which can be co-ordinated with or, still more, subordinated to the economy of Germany. Both culturally and economically Vienna will change into a provincial German town, a superior Linz. But then Linz and not Vienna was Hitler's home and spiritual *milieu*. And he will have truly performed his work: he will have destroyed a civilization which his own class and people had not created and which they had hardly appreciated. Possibly they will be happier without it.

PALESTINE AND THE BRITISH EMPIRE

[This memorandum was written for private circulation in November 1936, and is now published for the first time. Some confidential information and some detailed proposals have been omitted; otherwise, barring verbal or stylistic changes, it stands unaltered.

A non-Jewish Zionist, to whom I showed the memorandum recently, suggested that I should give it the heading of " Might-have-beens." It certainly looks like it after the Palestine Conferences. Still, I do not consider its contents to be of merely antiquarian interest. Men are apt to go off at a tangent, or to engage in political and moral acrobatics; but these seldom make history. History is determined by the basic, enduring facts of a situation. It often follows a spiral road: the same point is never crossed twice; history does not exactly repeat itself; but the same landscape recurs, seen from different levels.

The fate of Jewry is bound up with that of the British Empire, now more closely than ever: a defeat of the British Empire at the hands of the dictators would spell annihilation both to European and to Palestinian Jewry. If there is war, whoever fights Hitler and Mussolini will have the fullest support of every free Jew, of whatever nationality. It was therefore Arab support which it was deemed necessary to acquire at the Palestine Conferences; Jewish

84

rights in Palestine were to be the price (though in a world war the Arab States will clearly be moved by other considerations). The grief and agony of a persecuted, despoiled, helpless people, now threatened with the loss of its last hope and of its most holy possessions, counted for nothing. All the sacrifices were demanded from us, and all the gains were offered to the Arabs; we said that the sacrifices were excessive, the Arabs that the gains were incomplete; and then we were described as equally "unreasonable."

At the same time, the prime movers in these transactions seem to have tried to hide their true nature even from themselves. "Expediency" was coupled with a profession of newly discovered principles. There was stretching of consciences and twisting of arguments; and for fear of having to sin against the light, an attempt was made to put out the light altogether.

But the Balfour Declaration will survive all this feverish, naive, assiduous nibbling; it declares things that were and will be; and the light shall not be put out. Neither the British nation, nor even the British Government, has yet said its last word. Further, the true value of the "purchase" on the one hand, and the deeper common interests of nations on the other, have still to be tested by reality. Meantime we think of the friendship and help extended to persecuted Jews by the British people, given to them as victims of cruelty and injustice, not on grounds of expediency, and not to be withdrawn as a move in a political game; gifts infinitely precious in terms of the heart and the spirit. These will be remembered long after the Palestine Conferences are forgotten.]

THE Arab aim is national independence. Unless Great Britain abandons the strategic base which Palestine offers for the Suez Canal, and gives up Haifa Harbour, the pipe-line, and the aerodromes, she must face the fact that whenever she is involved in an international crisis, the Palestine Arabs will come out on the anti-British side; not necessarily from sympathy for the enemy, but because Britain and France are in control of Arab territory.

2. Even were there no Balfour Declaration, Great Britain could not expect a different attitude from the Arabs, or more gratitude, than she has received from the Egyptians and Indians. The Jewish National Home, if anything, makes the Arabs wish to appear more friendly to Great Britain than they are; for by putting all the blame on the policy of the Balfour Declaration, they seek, and often gain, British support and sympathy. These have encouraged the Arabs in their intransigent opposition to the Mandate, and have formed the greatest obstacle in the way of an equitable Jewish-Arab understanding based on the Mandate; which agreement is also in the interest of the Mandatory Power.

3. None the less, an understanding of some kind the Jews could have with the Arabs at any time were they prepared to act disloyally towards Great Britain. The Arabs object at least as much

to the Jews as " pacemakers for British Imperialism," as they object to Great Britain as the " guardian " of the Jewish National Home; they wish the Jews to throw in their lot with the Arabs against Great Britain and France. They understand the close connexion between the interests of the Western Powers and of the Jews, and therefore try to divide them and to play off one against the other, with a view to defeating both.

4. There has undoubtedly been Italian money, arms, and influence behind the Palestine riots. This does not mean that Mussolini is hostile to Zionism as such; but he, too, is hostile to the co-operation between Great Britain and the Zionists, and one aim of the Italians in inciting the Palestine Arabs and raising troubles with which they expect the British to be unwilling or unable to cope, probably is to make the Jews wish for a ruthless military Power as Mandatory, which would know its own mind, understand its own interest, and not hesitate to enforce respect and obedience. Even after the riots had broken out, representative Italians were still holding out (ineffectual) blandishments to the Jews. If Italy had obtained the Mandate, she would have settled two or three million Jews in Palestine, trained and armed them, so as to have a white army of some 300,000 men to hold for her the key position in the Eastern Mediterranean.

5. At present, men who are British subjects or who served in the British Army during the war, hold the chief posts in the Jewish Agency for Palestine. But even were there not a single British Jew in Palestine or in the Zionist Organization, the Zionists, in their own interest, would still have to wish for the British connexion, as the most suitable and advantageous for the Jews so long as the British Government does not flagrantly violate the spirit and letter of the Balfour Declaration and of the Mandate. Even if the Jews were two millions strong, with a million Arabs in Palestine, and surrounded by Arab States, they could not stand alone in the cockpit of the Mediterranean. But a connexion with a Power which has no Mediterranean interests would be useless; no one will make sacrifices or even conduct a sensible policy where he has no interests. A connexion with a Mediterranean power — France or Italy — would be supremely dangerous, as it would drag Palestine into every Mediterranean conflict. Great Britain has a first-rate interest in the Mediterranean, but it is of a " transit " character; it is unaggressive.

6. Moreover the Latin colonial systems follow that of Rome; they Gallicize or Italianize. Under a French Mandate the French language and the tricolor would be imposed on the Jews in Palestine, and the Paris stamp would be pressed on their nascent neo-Hebrew culture; under an

Italian mandate, they would have to give the Fascist salute and pass once more under the Arch of Titus. The British, if anything, do too little to encourage the English language in Palestine, and certainly do not, in any way, interfere with the Jewish cultural development.

7. Similarly, at a later stage, when Palestine is fit to constitute a self-governing unit in a wider federation, the British Commonwealth offers to the Jews a suitable framework, such as no other European state or empire could offer.

8. Even if the Jewish National Home were the chief or the only cause of friction between the British and Arabs, it could not be wiped out any more; and in its present condition it is sufficiently big to be an irritant, but not sufficiently strong to be a bulwark. It may be difficult to swop horses mid-stream; still less advisable is it to dismount and sit down in the middle of the stream. It is an essential British interest to get the Jews as quickly through the danger zone to the opposite shore. The Italians understand what a powerful asset the Jews could be for them in Palestine; it is high time that the British, or at least those who care for the British Empire, understood the use to which the Jewish National Home might be put by them. The present policy courts disaster for the British and Jews alike. If the Jews are left weak in numbers, unarmed and unprepared, who will stop

the Arab onslaught against them and the British whenever Great Britain finds herself involved in an international crisis?

9. The Jewish immigrants into Palestine are sometimes described by people who have no real acquaintance with them as " the scum of Eastern and Central Europe." Were they scum, when exposed to the recent Arab attacks, they would have fled from the countryside into the towns, or would have indulged in easy and indiscriminate reprisals. They did neither; and their record during these disturbances (to which British Police and Army officers can bear witness) proves their value as material for a military force. Nor does the spirit of Jewish urban workers in Palestine differ from that of the rural settlers.

10. No arrangement between the Jewish Agency and Great Britain, provocative to the Arabs, is suggested; this would be neither in the British nor in the Jewish interest. All we ask is that the British authorities should understand and appreciate our work and its possibilities, and not place unnecessary obstacles in our way, but, wherever it is possible, help us. Our immigrants to Palestine should receive military training. Colonies might be placed in such a way as to cover essential strategic points and lines. And last but not least, we could create an armament industry in Palestine, or at least industries which

might easily be converted for that purpose; in the first place, iron and steel works, engineering shops, and a chemical industry. Even if Cyprus should serve as a naval and air base, it will never be possible to develop it industrially in the same way as Palestine. The Hitler régime supplies us, in the German-Jewish refugees, with the best scientific and industrial experts at ludicrously low wages.

11. Jewish prosperity in Palestine ultimately depends on the Jews reaching an understanding with the Arabs. They cannot be truly safe, even if they are a majority in Palestine, with a vast and discontented minority in their midst, which can, moreover, appeal for help to the surrounding countries. We Zionists are therefore prepared to offer to the Arabs everything that can in reason be expected from us — economic advantages (which they have admittedly reaped to the highest degree during the last seventeen years), cultural help, political parity irrespective of numbers under the permanent guarantee of the British Crown — neither race must ever be reduced to a " minority status " in the land which they own in common. Nor could we admit any limitation on Jewish immigration into Palestine other than that inherent in the economic position; we must be allowed to develop the resources of Palestine and to bring in immigrants to the limit of the absorptive capacity of the country. With regard to land, we

are prepared to do all that can be reasonably done to prevent in future any " displacement " of Arab cultivators, however small it has been proved to have been in the past, and however much it was over-compensated by a very marked improvement in the condition of the rest. But land legislation must not be of a character which would prevent us from settling on the land and developing the agricultural resources of Palestine; in other words, it must not be of a political character, merely calculated to circumscribe the Jewish National Home. There can be no National Home without men and land, and political limitations on immigration and land purchase are clearly inadmissible under the Mandate. Naturally, the Arabs would like the Jews to remain an insignificant minority, at their mercy, to oppress and exploit, and to despoil and drive out, if ever the chance offers. And they will not consider a reasonable compromise, so long as the Jews are weak and some British officials almost openly work against them.

12. To sum up: British and Jewish interests in Palestine have by now become inseparable, and while the Jews require British protection and support, they can best defend British interests in that key position which Palestine forms in the Eastern Mediterranean. To do this, numbers are required; Jewish immigration must be encouraged, or at least not discouraged; the men must be well

selected, trained to arms, and properly equipped.
The Jews desire the friendship and direction of
the British military authorities. At the same time,
it is neither in their, nor in the British, interest
that the Arabs should be antagonized. If the
Jews had firm and quiet support from the British
authorities, they could reach an understanding
with the Arabs which would be both in the Jewish
interest and in that of the British Empire. The
Jews can develop an armament industry in Palestine which would serve the British forces in the
Mediterranean and possibly throughout the Middle
East. In spite of their best will and most
strenuous endeavours, they can be of no real use
to the British in Palestine unless they are trusted;
and, in turn, they cannot effectively co-operate
with the British authorities unless they can trust
these authorities. But they know that an influen-
tial section of the Palestine Administration is un-
friendly to the Jews, and an even greater number
indifferent; and that comparatively few Palestine
officials fully envisage the British Imperial interest
in Palestine. In these circumstances, the Jews
continually have to be on the defensive, suspicious
and anxious, and debarred from giving all the
help which they desire to give.

93

"SO YOU MAY KNOW FROM WHAT SORT OF PEOPLE YOU HAVE SPRUNG"

(" Observer," April 2, 1933)

Dr. Shmarya Levin once said, when comparing Jewish emigration to America with that to Palestine, that of the millions who went to America everyone was thinking about his own future or that of his family, while of those mere tens of thousands going to Palestine, everyone was concerned with the fate and future of the nation. Now in his own case it is clear that wherever he went, the Jewish people was first and foremost in his mind; and it is this which imparts to his autobiography — of which " The Arena " [1] is the third volume — its peculiar character. It is written with sincerity and directness, and turns on the incidents of his own life; none the less, even with regard to the most personal matters, he is conscious of being just one of his people — what has happened to him must have happened to thousands, nay millions, of Jews; they must have developed, suffered, hoped, erred, and striven,

---

[1] " The Arena," by Shmarya Levin.

as he has, and for similar, or even the same, reasons; so it is their history which he writes, and he develops its philosophy. And even in this he is typical: I remember how once, after an anti-Semitic riot, when I tried to discover what had happened from one of the victims, he, standing on the ruins of his looted, gutted house, insisted on discussing with me the fate and future and the sufferings of our people.

The present volume of Dr. Levin's auto-biography covers the years 1890–1905, spent by him in Warsaw, Grodno, Ekaterinoslav, and Vilna, as a rabbi and a teacher, and finally in Petrograd, as a Member of the First Duma. Geographically, it covers the main divisions of the old " Jewish Pale " of Russia — Poland, White Russia, the Ukraine, and Lithuania. Historically, it starts in the days of the systematic, ruthless, openly avowed persecutions under Alexander III; deals with the rise of political Zionism, and the gradual mental and moral awakening of East-European Jewry; and closes with the hopes raised by the apparent beginnings of a constitutional régime, and with their frustration. The world described in the book has perished; for the millions who remained in Russia it has been destroyed by Bolshevism, for other millions it has vanished in transplantation. It seems hardly credible that only a single genera-tion separates the Jewish-Russian parents from their American children — it is as if at least two invisible generations had been interpolated between them:

> For the great-grandchildren of their own parents, I would like to tell . . . through . . . the life of one person, what was the manner of life of those parents, so that the younger generation may have . . . some notion of their own origins. It is well, too, that they should know this much: the world of their parents beyond the eastern shores of the ocean was a many-sided world, rich in content, rich in colours, with deep economic foundations and abundant streams of spiritual life. It is not good for a young generation to be too proud, and to think that the world begins with it.

Dr. Levin reasons and argues, tells stories and parables, and keeps to human affairs and values; there is no room for impressionism or elaborate descriptions. Still, he has seen and watched the surrounding world, and occasionally in a flash a picture arises, the more striking because unpremeditated and simple. · Thus he writes, when about to move to Ekaterinoslav, a new town in the industrial and mining belt of the Eastern Ukraine:

> I had been accustomed for a long time to Lithuania, an ancient land, with ancient

96

cities and villages; the dust of generations lay upon it, and the worry of old age was like a visible shadow — it was a land that looked backward . . . beginnings were no longer made; men could only continue what the anonymous and forgotten past had begun.

But there, in the south, on the River Dnieper,

had sprung up, as under a magician's wand, the marvellous city of Ekaterinoslav. It is a city as broad, as open, as kingly, as the Dnieper itself; a city that takes its character from the mighty river and from the broad, powerful earth of the Ukraine.

And here is his farewell to his home, after his father's death:

This was my last visit to Swislowitz. I never saw the village of my birth again. I said farewell to the people, to the rivers and fields and forests, and in my heart thanked them for the marvellous memories of childhood with which they had filled all my life.

There are gems of definition and thought in the book which the reviewer feels tempted to quote; but they should not be torn out of their context, and I limit myself to one disquisition on Jewish philanthropists, which in reality applies to Jews and non-Jews alike:

It is a common characteristic of the man who has no long family tradition of business or public affairs behind him, the man who has carved out his own career . . . that he develops an extreme degree of self-confidence. Frequently enough, his self-confidence becomes megalomania; such men become gods in their own eyes. If they take an interest in public affairs, they imagine that their wealth entitles them to have the first and the last say. . . . They . . . believe that success in business entitles them to the rôle of spiritual leaders.

During the many years of my public and national activity, I have had occasion to meet many rich Jews, some of them wonderfully good and gentle persons, always ready to help their people in a big way. Their good intentions never came to anything, for God, who blessed them on the one hand with the means, punished them on the other with the ambition to possess a philosophy all their own. And their lean philosophy used to eat up their fat donations, as the lean cows in Pharaoh's dream ate up the fat cows, and of the latter we are told " it was as if they had not been."

" The Memoirs of Glückel of Hameln " [1] is a much older and much simpler book. She lived

[1] " The Memoirs of Glückel of Hameln," translated by Marvin Lowenthal.

in Germany in the second half of the seven-
teenth century, and on the death of her much
beloved husband — " the crown of my head "
— was left with eight young children, and other
four who, though older, still " stood in the
bitter need of their faithful father." She then
started, for her " heart's ease," to write these
memoirs.

The book is most touching in its simple piety
and warmth of feeling, and is written without
any conscious philosophy, certainly without any
thought that its pages, scribbled by a poor widow
in sleepless nights, might ever be printed and
become something of a classic. But in certain
ways these memoirs come curiously near Dr.
Levin's autobiography:

> I am writing down these many details,
> dear children mine, so you may know from
> what sort of people you have sprung, lest
> to-day or to-morrow your beloved children
> or grandchildren come and know naught of
> their family.

And this is how Glückel describes her parents:

> As for my father, no man had a greater
> trust in God; and if it hadn't been for the
> gout, he would have further increased his
> fortune.

After his death,

> often my dear mother had nothing but a
> crust of bread the livelong day. She never
> complained, but put her faith in God, who
> had never forsaken her. To this day she
> has kept her trust in the Lord; I would I
> had her disposition. But God endows each
> of us differently.

But in truth no one can accuse Glückel either
of lack of faith or of lack of charity. Here are
her thoughts on a transaction in which she and
her husband suffered great and undeserved losses.
The man who wronged them

> must have thought he was right and asking
> no more than his due; otherwise he would
> not — perhaps — have behaved as he did.
> Yet it went hard on my husband. But who
> could have helped him? " Who prays for
> what is past, prays in vain."
> And the good Lord, who saw our
> innocence, bestowed on us, e'er four weeks
> had passed, such excellent business that we
> close repaired our losses.

And it is thus that Glückel of Hameln, in her
own manner, from her own tiny corner, sums up
Jewish history and hopes:

> So from time to time we enjoyed peace,
> and again were hunted forth; and so it has

been to this day and, I fear, will continue in like fashion as long as the burghers rule Hamburg. May the Lord, in the abundance of His mercy and loving-kindness, have compassion on us and send us His righteous Messiah, so that we may serve Him with all our heart and once more offer our prayers in the holy Temple in the holy city of Jerusalem! Amen.

UNDER THE GEORGES

THE END OF THE NOMINAL
CABINET

("*Manchester Guardian,*" *June* 11, 1937)

ON February 14, 1921, King George V presided
over a Cabinet Council, attenuated and atrophied,
held to hear the Speech with which Parliament
was to be opened on the 15th. But no one present
seems to have known that this was a Cabinet
meeting, and when in July 1921 the King was
leaving for Scotland before the text of the Speech
could be conveniently fixed, it was decided to dis-
pense with a formality of which the origin and
meaning were forgotten — the Speech was to be
" sent to Balmoral in a box." The last vestige of
a Cabinet held in the presence of the Sovereign
was being extinguished, apparently without anyone realizing it.

While the outlines of the eighteenth-century
Cabinet have by now been drawn, the detail, which
in parts is of decisive importance, has still to be
filled in; and the subject calls for a film, perhaps,
rather than a picture to render the quick, fleeting
changes. No schematic pattern can do justice to
the history of the Cabinet, even in reference to

short periods. The last trace of life has to be removed from matter before crystallization becomes possible; but the Cabinet is a living organism, governed by the purposes which it serves, and has therefore always been essentially pragmatic in its nature. Whatever part of it is fixed tends to become ornamental, and in time passes into pageantry and folklore.

The story which ascribes the King's withdrawal from the Cabinet to an accident — George I's ignorance and George II's imperfect knowledge of English — is a crude and, by now, exploded legend. George II talked English to his Ministers, and notes in his own hand testify to his having had quite a satisfactory command of the language; while the thirteen years of George I's reign would not have wrought such a change had not deeper forces been at work, one of them being the gradual transference of the real business of the Cabinet to a new body. From the Cabinet Council over which the King had once presided he never completely withdrew, but that Council itself gradually faded away, till it sank into an anonymous grave, on which this essay is intended to place a commemorative inscription.

Early in the eighteenth century the Cabinet Council consisted of the Archbishop of Canterbury, the Lord Chancellor, the Lord President of the Council, and the Lord Privy Seal; the four great

Court officers — the Lord High Steward, the Lord Chamberlain, the Groom of the Stole, and the Master of the Horse; the Lord Chief Justice; the First Lord of the Admiralty and the Commander-in-Chief (or the Master-General of the Ordnance); the Lord Lieutenant of Ireland; the First Lord of the Treasury and the Secretaries of State; and a few more peers or statesmen summoned because of their personal weight. This was a Council of State rather than an Administration; it represented the Church, the Law, the Court, the Services, and (at the tail-end) the chief departments of State. Even when fundamental problems of policy were still debated and settled by this body, the working Ministers had to meet apart for the handling of current business — diplomatic correspondence, dispositions of the fleet or army, colonial or trade affairs, and so on. This smaller Cabinet necessarily included the First Lord of the Treasury, the Secretaries of State, and almost invariably the Lord Chancellor and the President of the Council, with others added according to requirements — for example, naval business could hardly be discussed without the navy being represented. But its composition was extremely elastic and pragmatic, and curious hybrid forms were developed at times. The one person who never joined the Ministers sitting, as it were, in their shirt sleeves was the Sovereign;

he never dropped out completely from the original Cabinet, but he never entered the one from which the present Cabinet is lineally descended.

By 1760 the original Cabinet had declined so much that it came to be called the " Nominal Cabinet "; while the smaller body of working Ministers was known as the " Efficient " or " Effective Cabinet," its members being referred to by names such as " the King's principal servants," " the King's confidential servants," or " the lords whom the King entrusts with his private correspondence " (they alone had the " circulation of papers," which is always the distinctive mark of the directing body).

The Nominal Cabinet seems to have retained only two regular functions, both performed in the presence of the King. It met some days before the opening or prorogation of Parliament to hear the King's Speech, and was occasionally summoned to advise the King on death sentences (this is why, in July 1766, Lord Temple, in a moment of irritation, contemptuously dubbed it " the hanging Committee "). As a special decision had to be taken to hold a meeting for hearing a criminal case, there is more material about this kind of Cabinet than about meetings for the King's Speech, which were apparently a matter of routine; moreover, as the King was present, a Cabinet minute, which usually took the form of a communication to him, was not required. Still, there is sufficient evidence to prove the existence of the custom.

To give a few examples. On April 23, 1755, Lord Hardwicke wrote to the Duke of Newcastle:

> Lord Chancellor sends his compliments to the Duke of Newcastle, and begs the favour of his Grace to make his humble excuse to the King for his not being able to attend the Council for the Speech.

On Thursday, November 13, 1760, before the first opening of Parliament in the new reign, Newcastle wrote to Hardwicke: " When is the Council to be for the Speech?" Hardwicke replied: " The Cabinet for the Speech may be to-morrow, if there is to be one without the King. That, in His Majesty's presence, need not be before Monday." On Sunday, November 16, Newcastle received, from Bute, George III's famous addition to the Speech: " Born and educated in this country, I glory in the name of Britain "; and wrote to Hardwicke that these words had to be inserted in the Speech, " which is to be laid before the King to-morrow in Cabinet Council." Again, on January 10, 1766, Newcastle, having received a summons from the office of the Secretary of State " to attend His Majesty, this day, in his Closet," wrote to Rockingham:

As I know, it was only for the Speech; and as I had told the King, that I had seen, and approved the Speech, I was sure, His Majesty would be so good, as to excuse me.

A few days before Parliament assembled the Speech was read also at another gathering — by the Leader of the House of Commons to its " efficient men " or " men of business " — that is, the front-benchers (at that time usually not more than one or two members of the Efficient Cabinet were of the House of Commons). These were, in fact, parallel meetings — at least four-fifths of the members of the Nominal Cabinet were peers, and it included almost all the leading men on the Government side in the House of Lords; it would therefore have been sheer pedantry to have had another meeting of the front-bench peers for the same purpose. But that no particular con-stitutional significance attached to this meeting of the Nominal Cabinet is shown even by the fact that in November 1760 the Speech was read by Pitt to the front-benchers of the House of Com-mons on the night before the Cabinet Council met for it in the presence of the King.

At a later date, a dinner began to be held for the Speech, attended by the Cabinet, the Speaker, the junior Ministers, and the Under Secretaries, lords and commoners alike; also by the movers and seconders of the Address. It was discontinued in 1931 for reasons of economy. Now a cup of tea and a bun take its place, and, as this treat is not sufficiently attractive for Cabinet Ministers, who are acquainted with the Speech, they have dropped out, the tea-party changing into a " children's party." [1]

In time the Cabinet Councils for the Speech came to be tacked on to meetings of the Privy Council, but although the memory of their origin, meaning, and character seemed to have been lost they were kept distinct from the others. The question, however, who was entitled to attend the reading of the Queen's Speech and, still more, what constitutional importance attached to it seems at times to have puzzled Presidents of the Council and other Ministers.

On November 29, 1852, Lord Exeter, then Lord Chamberlain, wrote to the President of the Council (this document, as well as the next, is in the Privy Council Office, and is now published with the permission of that department):

I have had the honour of communicating the contents of your letter of the 15th inst to the Queen, and I have received Her Majesty's commands to inform your Lord-

[1] In November 1938, the Prime Minister being detained by urgent business, the Speech was, very appropriately, read to the junior Ministers by the Chief Whip.

ship that in future it is Her Majesty's pleasure the Clerk of the Council shall upon all occasions when the ordinary business has been concluded and Her Majesty's Speech is about to be read desire the Gold Stick to retire with himself, and that the only persons who have the privilege of remaining in the Council Chamber with the Ministers, are the Great Officers of State and the Groom of the Stole to His Royal Highness Prince Albert.

Again, on September 13, 1884, Sir C. L. Peel, clerk of the Privy Council, wrote to Mr. Gladstone:

> With reference to our conversation at Balmoral, I cannot find any trace in the records of this Office of the Sovereign's Speech to Parliament having been ever treated as Privy Council business. . . .
>
> There is no mention of the Speech itself in any list of Business or in the Minutes of the Privy Council.
>
> I imagine that the Royal Assent is signified by the fact that the Speech is always delivered either by the Sovereign in person, or by the Lord Chancellor "in the Sovereign's own words" under authority of a Royal Commission. . . .

When in 1921 the difficulty arose of fixing the King's Speech before he left for Scotland, Sir

Almeric FitzRoy, Clerk of the Privy Council, submitted the following memorandum (which is printed in his " Memoirs "):

There is nothing to show that any constitutional sanction attaches to the approval of the King's Speech after a Council.

It is certain, on the other hand, that such approval is no part of the business of the King in Council, and it appears probable that the practice is the result of convenience hardening into custom.

In the old days Councils were usually attended by a large number of Cabinet Ministers, and the moment, therefore, was favourable for a formal act of the Crown in combination with Ministers; but now, in normal circumstances, the Lord President is the only Cabinet Minister present, and, so far as the presence of a second is concerned, it has been due to my efforts to secure it, in order that the Lord President should have the countenance of a colleague if any alteration is required at the last moment.

It was only in my time that the authentication of the approved document by the Sign-manual was introduced, and, now that the practice is formalized, it is clear that the King's approval can be as regularly obtained in that way as for any other Act of State for which it is requisite.

On these grounds, I submit that, at the dictate of convenience, the King's approval of the Speech could be signified upon the document being sent to Balmoral in a box if Parliament has to be prorogued while he is there, the Prorogation Commission having been passed at the last Council His Majesty holds before his departure to take effect upon the day upon which the Royal Assent is given to the last Act of the Session in being.

To this Sir Almeric adds that Mr. Balfour accepted his view, " pronouncing very firmly upon the folly of Ministers tying themselves up with conditional formulae in matters where practice was merely dictated by convenience "; and that the King himself emphatically agreed,

> so that all difficulty disappears, and the King's Speech will be approved on despatch to Balmoral in a box, without the preliminary of a Council: a step which years ago Queen Victoria denounced as " revolutionary."

Perhaps Queen Victoria was right, after all, when she described the step as " revolutionary," but probably even she did not fully understand what it was that was to be buried, unceremoniously, in a red dispatch-box.

THE STUNTED GIANT [1]

(" *Observer*," *April* 10, 1932)

LORD CHESTERFIELD was the heir to a great political tradition; was a brilliant *raisonneur*, with a clear, incisive mind; had judgment and foresight; knew how to work, could speak, and could write; held two of the highest offices of State, and, when in Opposition, was one of its chief leaders; and mismanaged no task with which he was entrusted. He ought to have made a considerable figure in politics; and yet he proved, most undeniably, a failure. The letters to his son are, to a high degree, the unconscious record of his unavowed disappointment, and the sequel to it; where he had failed, his son was to succeed; instead of a coronet he had the bar-sinister — yet he must succeed. What good had all the inherited advantages been to Chesterfield? Perhaps he thought he knew by now where he had failed, and why; in the person of his son he meant to try once more.

[1] " The Letters of Philip Dormer Stanhope, Fourth Earl of Chesterfield," edited by Bonamy Dobrée.

I am going off the stage, you are coming upon it; with me, what has been, has been, and reflection now would come too late; with you everything is to come. . . . (October 12, 1748.)

His success in the world is now the only object I have in it. . . . (May 18, 1751.)

I hope, I wish, I doubt, and I fear alternately. . . . (February 16, 1748.)

With an insistence which at times rises into frenzy, he presses the boy to carry out the task along the lines he has drawn — like a ghost trying to make a living man do something he himself had omitted to accomplish, and which alone, when done, can free him from his agony. Before long Chesterfield was to know that he had failed a second time.

What were the reasons of his own failure? He was too critical, too fastidious, too consciously intellectual, and, with all that, shallow. He despised the thoughts, or " errors," of the generality of men (" the ablest . . . are only comparatively able, with regard to the still weaker herd "), but set a high value on the human mind as such — on his own mind. He had neither creative passion nor unity of purpose, and therefore lacked single-mindedness; and while ready to pursue an interesting line of inquiry or argument, he easily tired of drudgery — " a half lazy man." He was

not a fighter, nor a master-builder, nor had he
the personality of a leader; in fact, he did not
even apprehend of what weight personality is in
the affairs of men. To him Bolingbroke was the
ideal all-round man, and the shining verbiage of
his writings Chesterfield deemed worthy of being
" got by heart "; while in Pitt he singled out
the graceful action and harmonious enunciation —
" his periods are well turned, and every word he
makes use of is the very best." For " everybody
knows the matter almost alike," and " manner is
all in everything." Active contact with reality, on
the few occasions when it occurred, left a singular,
disproportionate imprint on Chesterfield's mind.
As a young man he was Ambassador to Holland,
which remained to him what Persia was to the
late Lord Curzon. In 1745–46, he was Lord
Lieutenant of Ireland, and ever after that country
engaged his interest and sympathy. There alone
had he achieved success; there he had held a
viceregal position; had been unhampered by
colleagues, never in competition with equals; and,
which may have preserved his success, he was
there less than a year. On his return to England,
as Secretary of State, he failed either to prevail
against colleagues whom he despised, or to co-
operate with them in a practical manner; and
soon gave up the Seals, with no loss to the public,
and with the determination never to resume office.

Chesterfield admired, and often quoted, Cardinal de Retz: " I can truly call him a man of great parts, but I cannot call him a great man. He never was so much so as in his retirement." Was there not a touch of self-identification in that description?

Lord Hervey has left a picture of Chesterfield which, though unpleasant, is no mere caricature. He writes:

> Lord Chesterfield was allowed by everybody to have more conversable entertaining table-wit than any man of his time; his propensity to ridicule, in which he indulged himself with infinite humour and no distinction, and with inexhaustible spirits and no discretion, made him sought and feared, liked, and not loved, by most of his acquaintance; no sex, no relation, no rank, no power, no profession, no friendship, no obligation were a shield from those pointed, glittering weapons, that seemed to shine to a stander-by, but cut deeply in those they touched.

Compare with this Chesterfield's warning to his son in 1748:

> Never yield to that temptation, which to most young men is very strong, of exposing other people's weaknesses and infirmities, for the sake either of diverting the company, or

of showing your own superiority. . . . If you have wit, use it to please, and not to hurt. . . .

Seventeen years later he wrote to his godson:

If God gives you wit, which I am not sure that I wish you, unless he gives you at the same time an equal portion at least of judgment to keep it in good order, wear it like your sword in the scabbard, and do not brandish it to the terror of the whole company. . . . The more wit you have the more good nature and politeness you must show, to induce people to pardon your superiority, for that is no easy matter.

And in another letter, which was to be delivered to his godson after his death:

Yes, I have been young, and a great deal too young.

Hervey says that Chesterfield's person was

as disagreeable as it was possible for a human figure to be without being deformed. . . . He was very short, disproportioned, thick, and clumsily made; he had a broad, rough-featured, ugly face with black teeth, and a head big enough for Polyphemus. One Ben Ashurst . . . told Lord Chesterfield that he was like a stunted giant, which was . . . really apposite.

119

Writing to his son, Chesterfield hopes that exercise will " lengthen you out a little "; and continually inquires about his teeth:

> Do you take care to keep your teeth very clean, by washing them constantly every morning and after every meal? (July 30, 1747.)
> I hope you take great care of your mouth and teeth. . . . I do insist upon your never using those·sticks, or any hard substance whatsoever, which . . . destroy the varnish of the teeth. . . .

According to Lady Cowper, Chesterfield used to keep his upper lip drawn down to hide his black teeth.

To Chesterfield " the most useful art of all," the highest, the greatest, was " the art of pleasing." " To please, is almost to prevail "; " he who pleases the most will rise the soonest and the highest." A man should please by his manners, his appearance, his movements, his demeanour, his address, his conversation; he should insinuate, ingratiate himself, even with the multitude, because with them is the strength. He should cultivate women.

> I began the world, not with a bare desire, but with an insatiable thirst, a rage of popularity, applause, and admiration . . .

this . . . made me attentive and civil to the
women I disliked, and to the men I despised,
in hopes of the applause of both. . . . To
men, I talked whatever I thought would give
them the best opinion of my parts and
learning, and to women, what I was sure
would please them — flattery, gallantry, and
love. . . . By these means I soon grew in
fashion . . . I gave the tone.

But was he truly successful? The advice he gives
to his son suggests different conclusions:

> Take the tone of the company that you
> are in, and do not pretend to give it . . . this
> is an attention due from every individual to
> the majority. (October 16, 1747.)
> . . . abstain from learned ostentation. . . .
> Wear your learning, like your watch, in a
> private pocket; and do not merely pull it
> out and strike it merely to show you have
> one. (February 22, 1748.)
> Take this rule for granted, as a never-
> failing one; that you must never seem to
> affect the character in which you have a mind
> to shine. (May 17, 1750.)

At one time Chesterfield's letters to his son
were considered immoral; and, in spite of their
brilliancy, they are certainly unpleasant. Almost
every point in them, taken singly, may be explained, defended, admitted, or even endorsed;

yet the cumulative effect is downright nauseating.
Carried out to any degree, Chesterfield's teaching
would change a man into a homunculus. He
asserts " that it is in every man's power to write
what hand he pleases." The same misconception
he applies to character and behaviour. Are there
some " layers " missing in Philip Stanhope's
" *beau vernis* "?

> Now, pray let me ask you, coolly and
> seriously, *pourquoi ces couches manquent-elles?*
> For you may as easily take them as you may
> wear more or less powder in your hair, more
> or less lace upon your coat.

Moreover, this varnish is to be variable:

> In the course of the world the qualifica-
> tions of the chameleon are often necessary
> . . . you should, to a certain degree, take
> the hue of either the man or the woman that
> you want, and wish to be upon terms with.

With " restless attention," Chesterfield constantly
examines how he could best contribute to Philip
Stanhope's improvement.

> I can tell you I shall always be correct-
> ing, and never think my work perfect enough.
> . . . (March 23, 1746.)
> I believe it would do you no harm if

you would always imagine that I was present,
and saw and heard everything you did and
said. (July 9, 1749.)

Remember that I shall know everything
you say or do at Paris, as exactly as if, by
the force of magic, I could follow you everywhere . . . invisible myself. (November
8, 1750.)

. . . above all things . . . remember
to join *the Graces*. . . . How cruelly should
I be shocked, if, at our first meeting, you
should present yourself to me without
them ! (March 8, 1750.)

. . . if I find you ungraceful in your
address, and awkward in your person and
dress, it will be impossible for me to love
you half so well . . . let your intrinsic merit
and knowledge be ever so great. (April 27,
1749.)

You must . . . expect the most critical
examen that ever anybody underwent. . . .
(March 11, 1751.)

The Graces, the Graces, remember the
Graces! (January 10, 1749.)

What were the reactions of the poor boy to a
hundred letters in this strain? Whatever there
was in him of independence and personality must
have revolted, while the desire to please his father
(or the fear of displeasing him) must have paralysed
him. We know that he grew up awkward and
shy, loud and *gauche*; could we not learn more

123

about him? Chesterfield undoubtedly kept his letters; if they are still preserved, why not print them? The birds are said to sing the praise of Heaven for the worms they find — "do the worms sing too, daddy?" asked a child on being told the story. We have long heard Chesterfield's song; I wish we could for once hear Philip Stanhope.

By the time Philip Stanhope had grown up — *mal formé* beyond repair — Chesterfield resigned himself to it; and remained a kind, attentive, tender father. But at this time starts the new series of educational letters to his godson. Their essential doctrines are the same; still the letters are clearer, purer, free of over-emphasis and of hysterical endeavour; a quiet, wise old man wishes to impart some of his experience to his successor. And next come Chesterfield's grandsons. On the death of his son, whose closest friend and confidant he had wished to be, he learnt that the son had been secretly married and had left children. The daughter-in-law, whom he would hardly have chosen and whom his son had hidden from him, Chesterfield treats with kindness and sympathy, and he writes to her affectionately about "our boys." A fine and lovable side comes out in the letters written by Chesterfield in the last ten or twelve years of his life. Had he, indeed, been merely "stunted"?

THE MEMOIRS OF LORD HERVEY [1]

(" *Observer*," *October* 4, 1931)

LORD HERVEY writes about himself: " His real business in London was pleasure, but as he always told the King, it was to pick up news, to hear what people said, to see how they looked, and to inform Their Majesties what was thought by all parties. . . ." In the " Memoirs " his rôle is reversed, and to men and women, unseen, un-known, unchosen, he recounts things learnt at Court; and he finds visible pleasure in that, neces-sarily posthumous, display, which satisfies his urge for creation, his desire for intellectual survival, and the need of some compensation for his own futile existence and its insincerity. In life he had to feign deference to " royal trifles "; now he has pinned them down, and sees them writhe and shrink; and he gives it as his excuse for recording them that

> the generality of readers have so much a
> greater curiosity to hear the words of Kings

[1] " Some Materials towards Memoirs of the Reign of King George II," by John, Lord Hervey. Edited by Romney Sedgwick.

than of other people that they are amused
with the very same things from the lips of
that consequence that would lay them to
sleep related from any other.

Hervey, the gigolo, ridicules his masters, and
establishes his contemptuous superiority over his
new public, of whose presence he seems intensely
conscious. He takes them to the places of their
snobbish dreams, to the seats of splendour and
power, where they enter with a reverential awe, an
avid curiosity, and an unconscious readiness to
befoul: and there he has arranged for them a
monkey-show.

But below his studied malice and literary
endeavour there is intellectual curiosity and an
outlook on history. He was interested in the
essence of things —

> trifling circumstances often let one more
> into people's tempers and characters than
> those parts of their conduct that are of
> greater importance, from which one fre-
> quently knows no more of their natural turn
> of mind than one does of their natural gait
> whilst they are dancing.

He wrote for those who

> look into courts and courtiers, princes and
> ministers, with such curious eyes as virtuosos
> in microscopes examine flies and emmets,

and are pleased with the dissected minute parts of animals, which in the gross herd they either do not regard or observe with in-difference and contempt.

His theory is that things great and small are done in the same way by people who do not differ in essentials; that there is very little foresight or design in history, and a great deal of accident; and that wisdom comes after the event, in accounts which are as fanciful as they seem plausible.

> I content myself with only relating facts just as I see them, without pretending to impute the effects of chance to design, or to account for the great actions of great people always by great causes.

The lowest of people " have five senses, and none of the highest I know of have six "; and the doings of men, great and small,

> are still the same game, and played with the same cards, the disparity in the skill of the gamesters in each equally great . . . and the only difference is their playing more or less deep, whilst the cutting and shuffling, the dealing and the playing, is still the same whether the stakes be halfpence or millions.

The great, inhuman outlines of history Hervey

did not see, but he realized that where the players are many, the game has to be simple. He writes about Lord Townshend:

> He loved deep schemes and extensive projects, and affected to strike what is commonly called great strokes in politics, things which, considering the nature of our government, a wise minister would be as incapable of concerting, without the utmost necessity, as Lord Townshend would have been of executing them, if there was a necessity.

And, speaking of the behaviour of another nobleman, he says that it

> would have been more extraordinary than all the rest, if it had not been for that great and common solution for the many otherwise unaccountable riddles in people's conduct, which was his being a great fool.

George II is a favourite object of Hervey's invective. The King wished to appear a hero and a lover, a man who knew his mind and kept his own counsels; here he is shown doing things " because he had once done them," as " incapable of being engaged by any charm but habit, or attached to any woman but his wife," looking " upon a mistress rather as a necessary appurtenance to his grandeur as a prince than an addition to his pleasures as a man," and as possessed neither of

" mental resolution," nor of political courage.
And this is how, according to Hervey, things were
done at Court:

> Sir Robert [Walpole] communicated
> this scheme secretly to the Queen, she in-
> sinuated it to the King, and the King pro-
> posed it to Sir Robert as an act of his own
> ingenuity and generosity.

About the Queen, Hervey writes in 1734:

> Lord Hervey was this summer in
> greater favour with the Queen, and conse-
> quently with the King, than ever; they told
> him everything, and talked of everything
> before him. . . . She called him always her
> " child, her pupil, and her charge "; used to
> tell him perpetually that his being so imper-
> tinent and daring to contradict her so con-
> tinually, was owing to his knowing she could
> not live without him; and often said, " It is
> well I am so old, or I should be talked of for
> this creature."
> Lord Hervey made prodigious court to
> her, and really loved and admired her.

And here is a description of her relations to the
King:

> . . . she looked, spake, and breathed but for
> him, was a weathercock to every capricious
> blast of his uncertain temper, and governed

him (if influence so gained can bear the name of government) by being as great a slave to him, thus ruled, as any other wife could be to a man who ruled her. For all the tedious hours she spent then in watching him whilst he slept, or the heavier task of entertaining him whilst he was awake, her single consolation was in reflecting she had power, and that people in coffee-houses and ruelles were saying she governed this country, without knowing how dear the government of it cost her.

But even her Hervey did not always spare. This is his account of the departure of the Princess Royal for Holland:

> Her father gave her a thousand kisses and a shower of tears, but not one guinea. Her mother never ceased crying for three days. But after three weeks (excepting post-days) Her Royal Highness seemed as much forgotten as if she had been buried three years.

His descriptions of the Prince of Wales, and of others he hated — and these were many — make one wonder how much to accept of his testimony; he himself wondered how much would be accepted:

> . . . no one who did not live in these times will, I dare say, believe but some of those I

describe in these papers must have had some hard features and deformities exaggerated and heightened by the malice and ill-nature of the painter who drew them.

But take the following passage:

> This conversation was interrupted by the Duke of Newcastle, who made his entry with as much alacrity and noise as usual, mightily out of breath though mightily in words, and in his hand a bundle of papers as big as his head and with little more in them.

I have spent years over the Newcastle Papers, and would not have done so were they as empty as Hervey suggests; and yet the picture bears an unmistakable likeness.

" Some Materials towards Memoirs of the Reign of King George II " is Hervey's own description of his book; " I look upon these papers rather as fragments that might be wove into a history than a history in themselves." But after two centuries Mr. Sedgwick finds " the duties of an editor of the Memoirs . . . comparatively simple," because " posterity has yet to write its own history " of Hervey's time, and it is therefore " seldom possible to correct or supplement him." What a gloss on our history-writing! And yet, this new edition is of the greatest value;

certain important passages of the " Memoirs,"
removed for reasons of tact and propriety by the
first Marquis of Bristol and Mr. Croker, have
now been restored from a copy which Mr. Sedgwick has found at Windsor Castle; and a truly
admirable introduction has been provided by him,
the best essay yet written on Hervey. A very
thorough and extensive knowledge of the period,
and a most minute, careful, and conscientious
study of the available manuscripts and of Hervey's
correspondence, form its foundation; while the
story of Hervey is told with the fullest understanding of his personality, and is discreetly adorned
with wit which itself has a Herveian, eighteenth-
century turn. There is something very peculiar
about that period in the way it affects us who
work on it; when Sedgwick and I meet, we talk
eighteenth-century gossip, and tell each other
funny stories about the Duke of Newcastle, and
laugh at the old man whom, somewhere at the
bottom of our hearts, we both love.

GEORGE III SPEAKS OUT [1]

(" *Observer*," *January* 18, 1931)

WHEN I once explained to a friend my idea of how biographies should be written — "Oh, I see," he remarked, " you would call in Scotland Yard and the Royal College of Physicians." In the case of George III, undoubtedly some assistance from the College is required, and as for " The Diaries of Robert Fulke Greville," an expert review by a Fellow specialising in mental diseases might have been most appropriate, for the greater part of the book — and the only one which is of any importance, interest, or value — consists of day-by-day accounts of the King's acute fit of madness, October 1788–March 1789.

George III had never been sweet-tempered or well-balanced or taciturn. But in October 1788 he became " more peevish than he used to be," and " now talked much more than usual, and spoke to everybody on strange varieties of subjects ":

[1] " The Diaries of Colonel the Hon. Robert Fulke Greville, Equerry to H.M. King George III," edited by F. McKno Bladon.

133

His incessant talking became at last so remarkable, that it was thought necessary to recommend H.M. to be a little more silent; his physician, Sir George Baker, accordingly hinted to him that it was essential to his health to be less frequent and earnest in his conversations.

During the next days the " incoherence in thought and expressions increased." Occasionally he tried himself to check his incessant talk; thus Greville writes on November 15, 1788:

> In the evening, sensible (without prompting) that he was talking very fast, he altered and spoke in the third person — " The King did so — The King thinks so," etc. This correction he thus explained: " I speak in the third person, as I am getting into Mr. Burke's eloquence, saying too much on little things."

But even such insight was of little avail; Greville notes on November 19 — to quote but one example — that " H. My. had talked for nineteen hours without scarce any intermission."

At first Greville avoids mentioning the contents of those rambling talks, and merely hints that there were subjects " which, had he been well, he probably would have concealed " (November 20); and that " every now and then " the King was

" talking much unlike himself, I mean indecently, which never was his practice while in possession of his reason " (November 23). But finally Greville recognized his duty as a diarist:

> It is painful to mark such details, but the real state of His Majesty's mind, from time to time, is an object of so much interest and importance, that the progressive circumstances connected with it cannot be withheld in fair narration, where continued memorandums refer to daily occurrences.

Things repressed by George III in his youth were coming up, or, to put it in Greville's words, " his clouded judgment now was running riot against that which nature had blessed him with in his unembarrassed days." He had renounced the women he had loved, had married one chosen from the Gotha Almanack, and had been faithful to her all these years. Now, in his ramblings, he declared that he did not love her and " that he preferred another." He talked continually about Lady Pembroke, calling her sometimes " Queen Esther "; wished to go to see her; and inscribed declarations of his love for her on playing-cards formally addressed to his doctors. On one occasion he asked Greville to go to the library

> and look for Paley's Philosophy, in which he told me I should find that tho' the law

said that man might have but one wife, yet, that Nature allowed more.

Even when he was well on the way to recovery, he would still refer to the subject of Lady Pembroke, though in a more restrained manner. After a visit from the Lord Chancellor Thurlow on February 22, Greville heard

> that H. My. told the Chancellor that he had had an attachment thirty years ago, and that on this the Chancellor had advised him to drop such ideas at fifty.

George III in his youth had talked of Hanover as " that horrid Electorate," and professed to loathe it — because it was the home of his hated grandfather; he " gloried in the name of Britain." During his illness he continually talked of " retiring to Hanover," declared that " he would leave the country, and then in great joy exclaimed ' Victoria, Victoria ' "; though on one occasion, when he heard of the difficulties which the French had in Martinique, he rejoiced and " then animatedly added that he was become an Englishman again." The idea of returning to Hanover — for George III's English attendants a most unmistakable symptom of madness — similarly persisted well into his recovery.

In short, mixed up with madness was a reversion to type. At a time when the strait waistcoat was frequently applied to the King, he declared to one of his doctors that " the late King of Spain was mad, but yet that he had his State around him, and that no King but the King of England could be confined in a strait waiscoat." How truly Hanoverian!

The stories of the strait waistcoat in Greville's " Diaries " are truly pathetic. The man who, even in his madness, declared that he was born to command, and not to obey, was constantly threatened, or restrained, with it:

> Dr. Willis . . . recommended him to be more calm, or that he would certainly talk himself into a strait waiscoat. (December 21.)
> During the disturbances of this morning the waiscoat was brought in and shown — but it was not put on. (January 18.)
> At one time he took his opportunity of complaining to Sir Lucas [Pepys] and me, of the situation of a King in a strait waiscoat (and he now not unfrequently wore a precautionary one under his coat) in a most affecting manner, and when Dr. Willis was out of the room he opened his waiscoat and shewed us the strait waiscoat taking down its long sleeves, and strings —
> After this melancholy display it was necessary to pull off his coat to set it to

rights again — He stripped and never shall
I forget the painful, and unpleasant sight —
Heavens! What a spectacle to see the dear
afflicted King standing in a strait waiscoat, and tucking up himself, the sleeves
and strings, until they might be wanted!!
(January 2.)

Robert Fulke Greville was truly attached to his
King: and that is the best that can be gleaned
about him from his " Diaries." He was Fanny
Burney's " Colonel Well-bred," and this, too, is
a quality with which he can be readily credited;
temperament, critical thinking, and a sense of
humour tend occasionally to interfere with the
results of good breeding, but his mind and character seem to have been fully innocent of any
such disturbing qualities. It would be difficult to
imagine anything more insipid and inane than the
account which Greville gives of his own life at
Court in 1781, when the American Revolution
was reaching its climax. " Ceremonies impres-
sively attended to in all parts," rides in the
country, their Majesties walking on the Terrace
at Windsor, tea at the Lodge, evenings closing
" with the usual harmony of the King's band " —
these things fill his time and mind. On one occasion he had " the honour of handing the Princess
Royal up one of the narrow staircases in the dark
and landed her in safety, without one false step ";

on another, the King at table " took the best possible care of me, and among other things, recommended me to eat some beef steaks which he was then eating himself, and which he thought excellent." His attendance as Equerry during that year formed " the happiest month of my life."

THE LETTERS OF GEORGE IV [1]

(" *New Statesman and Nation,*" *November* 26, 1938)

In February 1812, after more than half a century, the reign of George III virtually reached its term. There was no hope for his recovery, and his son was sovereign in all but name. A new reign in a new age: but it started with the old expectation of a consequent change of Government. Once more the Opposition was to be disappointed: the Regent did not mean to dismiss the War Ministry. The letter announcing this decision opens with a statement of his constitutional position:

> Altho I consider myself as under no obligation to explain to any persons the reasons which may, at any time, induce me to arrange, as I think best, for the public service, the administration of the Government. . . .

And it was necessarily in terms of the Regent's right freely to choose his Ministers that Whigs, who had expected office from his favour, formulated their reproaches:

[1] " The Letters of King George IV: 1812–1830," edited by A. Aspinall.   3 vols.

As the restrictions upon the exercise of the Royal authority by your Royal Highness have now ceased, from which you are enabled to form such an Administration as you conceive the best calculated for conducting the affairs of the Empire. . . .

For the last one hundred years every group or party had " upheld " the " independency of the Crown," when exercised in their favour; and denounced similar expectations in others as " attempts to storm the Closet." " I am convinced," wrote in 1812 the Duke of Northumberland, " that H.R.H.'s . . . decisive character will frustrate every attempt which arrogance, ambition, or folly may make to take him prisoner and bind him in fetters." In March 1827, Lushington, Secretary to the Treasury, when urging that Canning, rather than Wellington, should replace Liverpool at the head of the Government, wrote: " The Crown has an unqualified choice, and the present posture of our affairs . . . illustrates the wisdom of our forefathers, in leaving the appointment absolutely to the King "; while Canning inveighed against aristocratic " confederacies " and declaimed about " the real vigour of the Crown when it chooses to put forth its own strength."

The language and forms of politics had changed little since 1760. Only the " extinction

of parties," prayed for on every accession since
parties had come to exist, no longer figures in the
1812 edition of the catalogue of cant: its place
is taken by wishes for a " union of parties." These
were now acknowledged as a basic element in
British public life, and the real transition from
Royal to Parliamentary Government was preparing
in the minds of men and in the technique of
politics. For it is the mechanism of coherent and
disciplined parties which has gradually deprived
the Crown of that power to choose its Ministers
which in 1812 and 1760, no less than in 1714
and 1727, was ascribed to it by theory and con-
ceded by practice (with restrictions inherent in all
practice).

An observer, revisiting England after fifty
years in 1812, would probably have been struck
most by the growth of effective routine in Government, of maturity and skill, a sureness of touch
which people still lacked in his day; and now it
was needed, for there was so much more to do.
Everything had grown in size: the population,
the wars, the taxes, the Debt; Parliamentary
sittings were longer, though (Burke and Fox being
dead) perhaps not Parliamentary speeches. The
Effective Cabinet had reached a normal size of 14,
about double that of, say, 1765. They still wrote
Minutes to the Sovereign and described themselves as his " confidential servants," though he

called them already his " Cabinet." Within that
body there was a growing cohesion, and the consciousness of being the King's " responsible
advisers," without whom he could not, and must
not, act; George IV's character added poignancy
to this conviction and to the manner in which it
was occasionally expressed. The moral tone of
the Government and nation had risen since 1760,
that of the King and his family was lower in
1820.

Over a good deal of this correspondence lies
the stale reek of reckless and even sordid transactions condensed into debts and blackmail. The
Regent continues overspending while Ministers
exhort him that " most of the landed gentlemen of
the country are obliged to submit to losses and
privations as well as to retrenchment " (March
1816). The Duke of York goes on with his " unprincipled foolery," and George IV, when paying
£50,000 of his debts, writes to him on December 3,
1823: " . . . . had I myself continued on the
turf, etc., it might have been difficult, without
great inconvenience to the country, for me to have
fulfilled the high duties of my present station."
Other brothers, too, have debts, claims, or griev-
ances. The Regent's daughter, Princess Charlotte,
at the age of eighteen, owes " no less a sum to
different jewellers and dressmakers than £20,000
and upwards "; and letters and presents of hers

have to be extracted from the hands of a shady (illegitimate) cousin. The Duke of Cumberland complains that in England " every blackguard newspaper can at once ruin the character of a man "; but when he quarrels with his old mother, he swears " by the Lord, HER letters shall be made public " (about which letters nothing was unseemly except their publication). The King is blackmailed by ex-mistresses, quondam friends, creditors, journalists, etc. And when his secretary leaves his service, ample provision is made for him in a prophylactic way, but he is pressed to accept a colonial or a diplomatic post, Ceylon or Sweden. At times George IV seems, to use his own words, " almost distracted " by anxieties. Knighton writes to him on February 12, 1822:

> I trust that the Almighty will give you peace, and that your afflicted mind will cease to be tortured by the overwhelming inquietudes which have of late made such painful inroads on your health. . . .
> Do not let your mind, Sir, be tied down by fetters of apprehension; anticipate, I beseech you, no ill, for I will not believe that any is to happen us.

And George IV writes to Knighton about his worries on December 30, 1827 (most of it underlined):

. . . to you, and to you alone, dear friend, it is that I can and that I do look therefore for my relief, as it is you and you alone who can and who I am sure will (from your real affection and attachment to me) entirely put an end to them, and by your powerful exertions and means, crush and put the extinguisher upon that host of vipers and hornets, which seems in particular at this moment, to have congregated itself together and purposely, to sting me personally. . . .

This is a mere fraction of a sentence, and a fair sample of his style; for sentences of 100–300 words, of the most drivelling kind, abound in his familiar, and especially in his jocular, letters.

Fortunately George IV's letters to his Ministers are mostly in a different style, having obviously been drafted by his secretaries; how far their ideas were the King's own, it is of course impossible to tell, though some sensible and some silly remarks clearly bear his imprint. But the King's magnificent Memorandum written on the formation of the Goderich Ministry, is in Knighton's hand and is such as, in any age, a royal secretary or official would delight to write to noble lords:

The office [of Chancellor of the Exchequer] requires ability and not aristocracy . . .
The King will have those that are

proper for their business and if there be room after this — the Cabinet may if they please look out for ornaments.

Of the letters from the Ministers, those of Liverpool are precise and formal; Canning's brilliant, incisive, at times even boisterous — for instance, that about a peerage to be granted with remainder to the second son, a proposal which at first had appeared " strong " to him:

> . . . but . . . as the eldest son is repre-
> sented to be an idiot, and as it appears to Mr.
> Canning (after some recent exhibitions in the
> House of Lords) peculiarly desirable to avoid
> encreasing, among their Lordships, the num-
> ber of specimens of irregular understanding,
> in another generation. . . .

The relation of George IV to Canning and Canning's letters to him suggest a curious human side in the King's nature; or otherwise Canning would hardly have made, as he often did, an unusual addition to the ordinary form of address: " Mr. Canning presents his humble and affectionate duty to your Majesty . . ." Good deeds performed by George IV are on record in this correspondence, which covers eighteen years; but even in these the sincerity or depth of his feelings does not always appear in a convincing manner. Sometimes it is compassion for fellow-sufferers and fellow-sinners: " I am quite aware of the trifling objection to some of the fooleries of his past life, but who is exempt from some nonsense or other? "

THE RISE OF GEORGE CANNING [1]

(" *Manchester Guardian*," *November* 11, 1938)

AT one time it was tacitly assumed that the vital principles of Victorian monarchy, of its Cabinet, party system, and Parliamentary government, were present in the constitutional structure of the eighteenth century. Now we ask ourselves by what steps and what stages has the modern system arisen. How came the change in colour, the bending and twisting, or straightening, of lines, how did the new pattern emerge?

Some of these fine, gradual changes can be traced in Canning's unpublished letters and journal, extensively reproduced by Miss Marshall. His real aim, since his Oxford days, had been the House of Commons, " the only path," he said, " to the gratification of ambition." But he did not want " to be brought in by an individual," only by his leader (this was 1793, and the eighteenth century was waning). He imagined that the Prime Minister had any number of seats under his direct management (a delusion which the eighteenth century transmitted to its historians).

[1] " The Rise of George Canning," by Dorothy Marshall.

Pitt explained that " his patronage as a Minister was in itself . . . very small indeed," but that there were borough patrons " with some of whom his recommendation solely would operate." Canning inquired whether on certain points he would be free to differ from the Government, and was told that what was expected from him was " a general good disposition " towards it (a sound eighteenth-century rule). When the time came to think of office Canning applied for " immediate and ostensible employment," so as not to receive " publick money " without doing " publick duty " (although he knew full well that it required "stupid country gentlemen " to treat all sinecure places and pensions as " corruption "). He became Under Secretary for Foreign Affairs. This was no sinecure in the eighteenth century, for the Under Secretary had to do work now done by officials, and, as often as not, was himself an official.

In 1801 Canning followed Pitt into retirement. Parties were by now taking shape — what line were ex-Ministers to adopt towards their successors drawn from the ranks of their own party? At first they deprecated all " systematic and factious " opposition (a thing practised but not avowed in the eighteenth century), spoke of " temperate and considered " criticism, and echoed Chatham's old slogan (which neither he nor anyone else has ever managed to live up to), " Measures, not men." Canning soon grew restless. There was an end to the war, but not to Napoleon's conquests, encroachments, and provocations. Yet

> I think it must be peace — because it is obviously Bonaparte's interest not to go to war immediately and because our apes here are evidently determined to stave off the evil day as long as they can. . . .

War restarted on May 18, 1803. The papers laid before Parliament would show, averred Canning,

> that in October and November last we might have been stout with advantage — and were then cowardly, that it was because we had been cowardly that Bonaparte became peremptory — and that the war is owing therefore to our weakness and not to our courage.

Pitt, though he heartily despised " the incredible imbecility of the Addingtons," refused to " harass " or " press " them; " if we are never to argue prospectively for fear of danger," retorted Canning, " nor retrospectively because it can do no good — there is an end of Parliamentary discussion altogether." " The country must hobble on from bad to worse, and sink so low that a change must come too late to save it." Addington " will patch up a scurvy peace in the summer, worse than he has just escaped, and be Bonaparte's humble slave for the rest of his life."

> The times are too big for little counsels, little prejudices, and little arrangements . . . great things are to be done, and . . . talents must be had, wherever they can be got, to do them.

When at last Pitt divided the House against the Government, he was disappointed by the size of his following; because, as Canning writes,

> he chooses to calculate on principles, which he is every day finding, have no existence as motives of action in the house of Commons. He is disappointed because there were . . . no *converts*, no *convinced* country gentlemen, no honest good sort of people quitting the Ministry from a sudden flash of persuasion that they were neglecting the interests of the country. . . .

Such things happened in the days of Chatham; and his son, though only in the forties, cherished conceptions which had become obsolete.

CHURCH AND STATE IN
EIGHTEENTH-CENTURY ENGLAND [1]

(" *Observer*," *September* 1, 1935)

THE history of the National Church in the
eighteenth century is not the exclusive concern of
ecclesiastical historians or of students of religious
thought, for the Church was an essential branch
of England's national organization, and men in
Orders formed a high proportion of the intelligentsia; and it is the distinguished merit of
Professor Sykes's work that to a minute knowledge
of every aspect of the Church's inner life, he joins
a proper appreciation of her political tasks and
social affiliations. After the spiritual and political
upheavals of the preceding age, this was the time
of England's inner consolidation, when common-
sense and ready toleration — in other words,
insistence on a conformity of a singularly un-
exacting type — effected a reconciliation in this
country such as France was never to reach after
her great Revolution. To some, non-jurors or
" tender consciences " on the Dissenting side

[1] " Church and State in England in the XVIIIth Century,"
by the Rev. Norman Sykes.

may be more attractive, and they probably were intellectually more consistent, than the ecclesiastic statesmen of the Hanoverian period; but they might easily have plunged England into further civil wars, while the Church, such as it was, helped to heal the divisions and to reunify the nation.

Pluralism, favouritism in appointments, and laxity in the discharge of ecclesiastical duties, are the overt reproaches most frequently levelled at the eighteenth-century Church, almost as if such things had been unknown in preceding ages, or in the eighteenth century had been peculiar to the Church. (But when pluralism occurs in a man like Archbishop Sancroft, a non-juror, the glowing devotion of an admiring biographer makes it into a ground for praise — " a stronger proof can scarcely be afforded of the general estimation in which his character was held than by the fact of so many preferments flowing upon him, in this short space of time, from so many various quarters.") Pluralism was, to a large extent, the ecclesiastical equivalent of sinecures in the State — the Church could not but reproduce the dominant features of the national structure.

As to oligarchy, its extent in the eighteenth century has been greatly exaggerated, both in State and Church. For while a Duke of Grafton or a Lord Rockingham could attain high office without much work or merit, men like Walpole or Pitt towered far above them. Similarly, in between the prelates of noble family and extraction,

> there sat bishops such as Secker, educated first at a dissenting academy. . . . Warburton, who was a graduate of no University . . . and Maddox, whom Gibson fostered as an orphan in a London charity school. . . .

Dr. Thomas Newton, subsequently Bishop of Bristol, thus explained the theory of ecclesiastic preferments in a sermon preached at the consecration to the episcopate of William Warburton:

> Though the apostles, for wise reasons, were chosen from among men of low birth and parentage, yet times and circumstances are so changed that persons of noble extraction by coming into the Church may add strength and ornament to it; especially as long as we can boast of *some* who are honourable in themselves as well as in their families. . . .

And George Grenville distinguished two kinds of bishoprics — " bishoprics of business for men of abilities and learning, and bishoprics of ease for men of family and fashion."

Again with regard to nepotism (a form of favouritism objectionable so long as it remains merely an inept approach to heredity), a similar parallelism can be traced between Church and State. Lord Sandwich wrote, in August 1764, to a naval officer, about to quit in disgust at having been passed over:

> . . . as to Sir William Burnaby's making his son a Captain, it was very natural for him to do it. . . . I am satisfied in my opinion that no one has a right to complain that he has given his son the preference over every recommendation.

And a poor curate, displaying the virtue of humility, wrote to Archbishop Wake in 1724:

> I don't presume to find fault with the Bishop of Worcester for preferring his nephew. I only wish it were my good fortune to be a Bishop's nephew too.

As for laxity in the discharge of ecclesiastical duties, Professor Sykes's very extensive study of the life of a great many eighteenth-century prelates goes far to rebut that reproach and presents a picture of a good deal of honest, hard work done under difficult conditions. But

> at the heart of the problem of episcopal administration lay the distraction from the proper business of diocesan oversight in-

volved in the residence of bishops in London
during the greater part of each year.

Between 1715 and 1780 the House of Lords had
a membership of about 220, and an average attendance of 120-145; and the twenty-six bishops
" represented a not inconsiderable proportion even
of the numerical strength of the House." Attendance in Parliament on their part was a duty to the
State, no less than to the Church, " in an age which
saw so great an advance in the prestige and
authority of both Houses, and in which the House
of Peers played no insignificant part in debate and
legislation."

The saddest aspect of the eighteenth-century
Church (as also of the Army and Civil Service)
was the condition of the depressed subalterns —
curates and the unbeneficed clergy — who, even
after having overcome numerous initial obstacles,
still found the greatest difficulty in eking out a
subsistence. Here was an intellectual proletariat
such as we sometimes incline to think peculiar to
our own age. How modern sound some of the
contemporary remarks on the problem! Even in
the Caroline age, Bishop Stillingfleet

> wished to discover some means by which
> " the multitude of ordinations could be pre-
> vented, which had long been a great injury to
> the Church," since " there were at least

double the number of clergymen to the benefices and preferments in the kingdom."

And in 1711, Addison wrote:

> I am sometimes very much troubled when I reflect upon the three great professions of divinity, law, and physic: how they are each of them overburdened with practitioners and filled with multitudes of gentlemen who starve one another.

There is, unfortunately, no statistical estimate of the proportion which men in Orders formed of the eighteenth-century intelligentsia, though this could be obtained with the help of university and school registers.

AN EIGHTEENTH-CENTURY
TRAVELLER [1]

(" Manchester Guardian," September 13, 1934, *and*
June 24, 1935)

I

JOHN BYNG often wondered what it was that made
him travel — why people should leave comfortable homes and

> lavish their money abroad, hunting after
> idle pleasures, in which pursuit they are sure
> to encounter real miseries . . . and yet
> neither deters me nor others, from running
> wild about the world. . . .

He loathed uncomfortable beds, noisy inns, and
late suppers (" but being obliged to order, I think
myself obliged to eat "), stony roads and muddy
lanes, the hardships of pleasure parties and the
gloom of the unsettled life in watering-places.
At the end of his Tour, on July 6, 1781, he wrote:

---

[1] " The Torrington Diaries." Containing the Tours through
England and Wales of the Hon. John Byng (later fifth Viscount
Torrington). Vols. I and II. Edited by C. Bruyn Andrews.

> The imposition in travelling is abomin-
> able; the innkeepers are insolent, the hostlers
> are sulky, the chambermaids are pert, and
> the waiters are impertinent; the meat is
> tough, the wine is foul, the beer is hard, the
> sheets are wet, the linnen is dirty, and the
> knives are never clean'd!!

And this at the end of the third of the fourteen
Tours of which the record has been preserved:

> This will probably be my last expedi-
> tion of the kind. . . . I feel myself unequal
> to a daily worry, and a nightly change of
> beds; in consequence my nerves shatter, and
> my spirits tire. . . . Valetudinarians must
> live where they can command, and scold.

Formal parks, with " staring temples and
obelisks," so dear to the generation which had
immediately preceded his own, were not to his
liking; nor did he enjoy wild scenery and extensive views which his contemporaries were beginning to appreciate. He would not climb Cader
Idris: " I hate distant views; am giddy on heights;
and very hot and nervous." Even the Malvern
Hills were too much for him — his nerves felt
" much harrass'd, from being unused to such
heights and declivities." And about Leckhamp-
ton Hill he writes: " This is a truly fine prospect;
yet prospects please me but for an instant, for they

fatigue my eyes, and flurry my nerves, and I allways wish to find myself in the tranquil vale beneath."

Again and again the reader will ask himself — what is the curious attraction of this seemingly unattractive book? His descriptions of the things he saw are seldom vivid; while their enumeration is hardly illuminating where the ground he covers is unknown to the reader, and is meagre where it is familiar (though occasionally he will find interesting details about some particular place or building). Perhaps largest of all loom the problems of Byng's everyday existence — lodgings, food, and drink. They engrossed his mind and fill the pages of his diary, and their discussion is raised to the heights of a theory; for he objects to tours being written

> too much in the stile of pompous history; not dwelling sufficiently upon the prices of provisions, recommendation of inns, statement of roads, &c. so that the following travellers reap little benefit from them.

Byng supplies such information though he was writing for posterity only. He was determined that his diaries should not be published in his lifetime, but hoped that they would be read with avidity a hundred years hence,

> as descriptive of the manners of our travelling, the rates of our provisions; and of

castles, churches, and houses, that may then be levell'd with the ground.

He speaks with contempt about "those dirty, idle, memorials of Lilly, and Ashmole, who tells us of every shocking ailment that assailed him and how often he sweated, and purged"; from which his own account of the beds he lay in without sleep, and of the meals he consumed with oppressive results, are only one stage removed. Still,

> all diaries are greedily sought for, let them be ever so ill and foolish written, as coming warm from the heart.

His own diaries certainly come from the heart, a tortured, suffering heart. "I find every one more retired, perhaps wiser than myself; and not so leaky of secrets, and hasty of determination." Sociable by nature, he could not even entertain his friends with real pleasure; and describing a young host "of modest manners and easy deportment," he adds:

> I remark this, more particularly, as I suffer so much, and am allways (in spite of inward remonstrances) constrain'd, unhappy, and fluster'd at my own table.

How he wished for the "tranquil vale" and a real ease of mind! Here is happiness as he imagines it:

> . . . how I should like to pass a November in such a place and country with a sociable, hunting, whist party, and our own wine! To hold a good horse in my hand every morning; then a good glass of wine; and then a good quantity of trumps.

But on he went travelling; and much of the charm of his diaries lies in the contrast between the wish for peace and that restless curiosity which drove him on; between the shyness which determined him not to publish his diaries, and the desire that some day they should be read; in their simplicity and sincerity — " I am resolv'd to judge for myself and not follow the opinion of every gazer, and flatterer "; and in the discreet tolerance and practical wisdom of that inveterate grumbler. When he finds himself in the uncongenial atmosphere of his wife's family, he remarks: " As I was only to make a short stay (for I never sacrifice but one day of the year here) I behaved with acquiescence of temper." He praises music and card games because, though sociable, they save " the trouble of conversation." Even his diaries were an escape from controversial talks:

> My nerves have lately encouraged me to much writing, being not equal to violent argument, and contradiction, which ever flutter away my little capacity; and render

such opinions as may be reasonable, and wou'd sound decently upon paper, of hasty, and weak effect.

And thus in the worries and misery of his journeys, he tells, half unconsciously, about those of the much greater journey to which he himself sometimes compares them, wishing for the end of both, and yet clinging with infinite curiosity to what the world offered him.

II

Between 1789 and 1791, John Byng, in continuance of his travels, made two tours in the Midlands, one in Bedfordshire, and one in Lincolnshire. He had by now worked out a certain technique and his writing shows a growing self-consciousness — his memoirs, if they survive, will be read:

> I will now indulge in a little hasty vanity, and satisfaction, in thinking how pleasant my tours will be to readers, an hundred years hence. . . . Of all the tours I read I like my own the best (Well said, master!) because all others are so cramm'd with learned investigation, and new fangled drawings; perpersely to forward a sale, whilst all pleasure minutiae are left out, as unworthy of the public eye.

My pleasure in touring is not confin'd to time; (tho' that I enjoy as much as any man) but the completion of my journal furnishes me employ for the following winter, as I then dilate my former notes; besides the expectant pleasure of an old age perusal.

But the reader naturally wonders what are those minutiae of pleasure, or the enjoyment of touring, to a man so regularly displeased as John Byng appears in his Diaries. The tale of bad inns continues.

Several fat, stupid, female servants attended us . . . at our bad, ill-serv'd, supper.

. . . a most blackguard stop . . . some fat, greasy maids. . . .

My sheets were so damp, and the blankets so dirty and stinking, and the room so smelling of putridity, that I slept very little. . . .

My landlord, fat, stupid, and splay-footed. . . .

And so it goes on in endless succession. Once, and only once did Byng find an inn deserving of the highest praise; it was the Ram's Head, at Disley, a —

snug little, comfortable inn . . . a neater and more chearfully situated inn I never saw. . . . The stables are excellent; the brown bread, and cheese, so good; the water so cold; the decanters so clean; and the bed rooms so nice; that I wish'd to make a return, and pass more time here.

But, as if to make amends for such high praise, a few pages further, having entered a supremely nasty inn, he adds — " these petty miseries exalt something better into superlatives."

Nor is it clear where Byng finds any compensation for these " petty miseries." The country houses which he visits do not please him much more than the inns at which he stops; he dislikes Chatsworth; speaks of " the nasty stare-about Castle of Belvoir "; of the " mean entrance into Coombe-Abbey Park "; the " modern, red-brick, tasteless house " of Lord Stamford, at Dunham-Massey; and the " ugly, modern house " of Lord Hardwicke at Wimple. Mr. Okeover's place at Mapleton " tho' in a lovely vale . . . is kept in wretched taste "; Dunnington Park, of Lord Huntingdon, Byng mistook for a gardener's lodge; the seat of Lord Pomfret at Easton-Neston is " a great, staring, unpleasant dwelling, of neither comfort or content "; Sir Robert Burdett's, " is of vile architecture, and in a bad situation "; Sir Richard Arkwright's new house is " an effort of

inconvenient ill taste "; and Mr. Leigh's of Lime,
" is in the horrid taste, and manner of Chatsworth,
all windows," while his park " is a dreary waste,
abandon'd to rabbits." And so goes on the
rondeau of delights for the sightseer.

As for company in travelling, there are some
discreet hints of differences and mutual disgust:

> touring cannot be taken alone; and for
> company to go together becomes almost
> impossible.

> . . . cou'd touring in company be well
> understood, what satisfaction it wou'd afford!
> But people will pull different ways, and dis-
> dain a director; so schisms and wrangles
> quickly arise to disever acquaintance, and
> friendships, that might, otherwise, last long.

> To me, who feel every wish to move at
> my own taste, at my own hours. . . .

It seems obvious that on such companionable tours
Byng meant to be the " director." Was he happier when alone? Here is a significant passage:

> I had no one to speak to, my writing was
> quickly exhausted, and so I strove to think;
> but I (*now*) hate thinking; — I left London
> to avoid thinking; in youth, people won't
> think, and when they grow into years it is of
> no use!

166

Perhaps the chief purpose of his tours, except to give him " employ " afterwards, was to escape London and society — for he has not become more sociable as the years have gone by. And this is a typical *cri de cœur*:

> I seek not company, and noise; I turn not my head to look at a woman; for I leave London that I might see Nature in her wild, and most becoming attire. . . .

Indeed, " romantic " nature and romantic ruins, are what Byng seemed to enjoy.

> The appearance of this castle (Maxstoke Castle), so correspondent of romantic history, and legendary tale, highly engross'd my thoughts and attentions.
> A clear, surrounding, moat, an inhabited fortress of 60 yards square, turreted, and preserv'd with battlements; all this serv'd much to my inspiration!

And on another occasion:

> to me castles and monasteries in decay are the daintiest speculation.

Unfortunately even inspired speculation seemed never to call forth from Byng descriptions which could convey a vivid or pleasurable impression to the reader and therefore the book continues in its unrelieved gloom.

A new industrial England was growing up in the Midlands, nasty perhaps, but interesting; of which an account in those days would be welcomed. There is one, of a kind, but merely to complete the picture of displeasure:

> I abominate the sight of mines, and miners, as unproductive of pleasure; and the wretches who work in, and about them, seem devoted to darkness, dirt, and misery. . . .

> The silk mills [at Derby] quite bewildered me; such rattlings and twistings! Such heat, and stinks!

> Salford . . . where the noise, and drunkenness of the artisans quite overcame me, added to a long crawl over the stones.

> Manchester: this great, nasty, manufactoring town. . . .

Having visited Sunday schools at Stockport he writes:

> I am point blank against these institutions; the poor should not read, and of writing, I never heard, for them, the use.

And at Manchester:

And here let me (ignorantly perhaps) impetuously state my wishes, " That trade was unknown "; (or that I had lived when it was but little known).

He had some foreboding of terrible upheavals:

. . . a fear strikes me that this (our over stretch'd) commerce may meet a shock; and then what becomes of your rabble of artisans!

Lastly, here is a generalizing description of England in 1789:

. . . from my . . . observations . . . noblemen, and gentlemen have almost abandon'd the country . . . yeomanry is annull'd. . . . So, amongst the first great people, now residing there, may be reckon'd the inn keepers, the tax gatherers, and the stewards of great estates who with the lawyers rule the country. Justices . . . are afraid of the felons; constables are not to be found; the poor must plunder because not provided for; ladies dare not live in the country; taxes are evaded; enclosures of common field land, and commons, are general; corporations are venal; trade and manufactories are over strained; banks and bankruptcies in and over every town; laws, from being multiplied beyond comprehension, cannot be enforced; London markets and London prices govern the whole kingdom; and as that encreasing Wen, the metropolis, must be fed the body will gradually decay. . . there will come a distress, a famine; and an insurrection; which the praetorian guards, or the whole army cannot quell; or even the Parliament pacify. . . .

Had this been written about France in June 1789, how much would it have been quoted as a most remarkable prophecy, and an explanation of what followed.

SO COME AND JOIN THE DANCE...

An Eighteenth-century Political Transaction with a Dismal Conclusion

(" *Nation and Athenæum*," *June* 21, 1928)

Dramatis Personae

JOHN CALCRAFT was a well-known regimental agent; for a long time he was the right-hand man of Henry Fox, but deserted him in 1763. In 1757 he bought the estate of Rempston in the Isle of Purbeck, in Dorset, within walking distance of three Parliamentary boroughs, Corfe Castle, Poole, and Wareham, and set to work to capture them. He succeeded in having his brother, Thomas Calcraft, elected for Poole in 1761; in 1767 he purchased the Manor of Wareham from Thomas Erle Drax, " and also all the lands of George Pitt, John Pitt, and John Bankes, esqres, and almost all the freeholds in the borough soon after " (see Hutchins, " Dorset," vol. i. p. 82). He failed in his attempts at Corfe Castle, and gave up whatever footing he had gained in it to Mr. Bankes in exchange for his " interest " at Wareham; Corfe Castle had for a century been owned and represented by the two families of Bond and Bankes, and remained with them until disfranchised by the Reform Act of 1832.

The Fursmans, a West Country family, are mentioned by Hutchins at Wareham early in the eighteenth century. A Rev. John Fursman of Lamerton, Devonshire, appears in Joseph Foster's "Alumni Oxonienses," and died as Canon of Exeter Cathedral in 1757. William Fursman, to whom Calcraft's letters are directed, was a "waiter and searcher" at the Custom House at Deal, as can be seen from a letter of his to the Duke of Newcastle dated June 12, 1744 (Add. MS. 32703, f. 113).

The letters which follow are from one of Calcraft's letter-books at the British Museum (Add. MS. 17493). Fursman's replies are not extant.

(f. 96) John Calcraft to W. Fursman at Deal, October 3rd, 1757:

> Your very obliging letter of 28 September found me in Wilts on Fryday, or should sooner have been answered. You are very wise to provide for your son who, Captain Pool tells me, is a proper person for the Army, and if you will accept a pair of colours for him, I will immediately procure them. Should he dislike the Army, the Custom-

house place may in that case be applied for, which if it could be ever got might not be soon and 'tis pity the young gentleman should not at his time of life take to some profession. If the Army proves agreeable you may depend on my continued attention to him. I do not mean or wish to prejudice Mr. Bond but on the contrary hope to cultivate his friendship, and I hope you will allow me to purchase your burgages at Corfe. I shall be obliged to you for an immediate answer because I forsee a speedy opportunity of getting an ensigncy, if your son chooses it, and am, with great regard, etc.   J. C.

William Fursman's son obviously chose the Army, and on November 19, 1757 (f. 111), John Calcraft wrote to Lord Home, Governor of Gibraltar, for whom he was agent:

Ensign Fursman of Jefferey's [Regiment] will have the honour to deliver you this letter; he is son to a gentleman who is kind enough to give me his interest in a borough where I hope your Lordship will see either my brother or some other friend of mine chose next election, and is a very promising young gentleman. Wherefore I will earnestly recommend him to your Lordship's protection. . . .

But young Fursman does not seem immediately

to have started for Gibraltar, for on February 26, 1758, John Calcraft is found writing another letter to Lord Home for him with a new recommendation (f. 149):

> Fursman is a friend's son at Corfe Castle where I have an estate that I hope will in time give me some influence, so I will recommend him to your Lordship to shew him any little civility that lyes in your way.

This time Ensign Fursman started out on the " Prince George," Admiral Broderick's flagship, the squadron acting as a convoy to a numerous fleet of merchant ships bound for the Straits.

On May 15, 1758, John Calcraft wrote again to Lord Home (f. 166):

> What a terrible misfortune is happen'd to Broderick's ship on board of which was my poor friend Fursman who I doubt is lost as I hear nothing from him. He had a long private letter for you and when I shall have an opportunity to send you another I don't know.

Two days later, Calcraft, seeing his last chance of making capital of poor Fursman's " ensigncy," wrote to his father:

> I wish I could ease the anxiety your mind must be under but I am sorry to say

I cannot get any certain tidings about your son, the minute I have you shall know. Duplicates of all my letters recommending him shall be forwarded, I have already received answers to some in which I mentioned him, so doubt not but if it has pleased God to spare him he will be well received. If you will desire your friend at Corfe to support me in my undertakings there, you will oblige me. Make yourself, dear Sir, as easy as you can 'till you hear more of this melancholy affair and believe me always, etc.

Young Fursman was dead, for in a letter to Colonel Jeffreys dated June 4 (f. 172) Calcraft mentions that Mr. Bruen is " to succeed poor Fursman."

A full account of the disaster of the " Prince George " will be found in the " Gentleman's Magazine," vol. xxviii. (1758), pp. 228-30. The ship caught fire at sea in broad daylight and of a " complement " of 715 and 30 passengers to Gibraltar, 745 in all, only 260 were saved. The other ships seem to have feared to approach it, for " not knowing we had taken care to float our powder, were under sad apprehensions we might blow up " (letter from Mr. Parry, an officer on board the " Prince George "). The Rev. Mr. Sharp, the chaplain, gives an even more sinister account of what happened during that catastrophe on April 13, 1758:

> . . . More might have been saved had the merchantmen behaved like human creatures; but they kept a long way to windward the whole time; and if possible, to their greater shame be it spoken, instead of saving men that swam to their boats, they were employed in taking up geese, fowls, tables, chairs, and whatever else of the kind came near them.

NAPOLEON

HIS LETTERS[1]

(" *Manchester Guardian*," *August* 6, 1934)

NAPOLEON's correspondence is practically all pragmatic in character; he had no time and no mind to engage in theoretical disquisitions or purely intellectual pursuits; he wrote to gain over, to command, or to reprove people — and an unprincipled man does not appear at his best when trying to captivate, nor a giant when chiding small men and showing them his contempt. Napoleon's greatest deeds were in direct action — things done, and neither analysed nor discussed; and perhaps his kindest deeds consisted in silent forbearance: he heaped benefits on relatives, friends, and collaborators, however low he valued them, and dismissed them unpunished when he knew that they were betraying him.

The best type of his writings is thus described by himself in September 1802:

> Every word in my proclamation [concerning Switzerland] speaks volumes: there

[1] " Letters of Napoleon," selected, translated, and edited by J. M. Thompson.

179

is not a syllable of rhetoric in it: it expresses exactly what I mean. My policy is honest and above-board, for it springs from long meditation backed by force.

And here is his theory of how a Government should speak, explained to his brother Joseph in April 1807 on the dissolution of monasteries in Naples:

> Documents dealing with religious matters should be expressed in language of a religious and not of a philosophical tone. There lies the art of statesmanship, and it is one that an author or a man of letters does not possess. . . . It is easier to put up with unpleasantness from a man of one's own way of thinking than from one who takes an entirely different point of view. . . . I think poorly of a Government whose edicts are always literary compositions. The thing is to give each edict the style and character of the special subject to which it applies. An educated monk who believed in the suppression of monasteries would not express himself as you have done. Men put up with injury if it is not accompanied by insult and when the blow does not appear to have come from the enemies of their profession.

There is an art in such adjustments which, if

180

they answer the purpose, tends to eclipse their meanness. But when in Egypt Napoleon tried to write like a Mohammedan, and inveighed against the Turks for their alliance with " believers in three gods," or when, in 1809, he attacked the Papacy for " becoming allies of the Protestants and of the enemies of Christ," his performances were both low and clumsy. In his innermost mind Napoleon had all the " depreciation of religion " peculiar to the age of " enlightenment " without its appreciation of intellectual values.

> People complain [wrote Napoleon in November 1806] that we have no literature: it is the fault of the Home Minister. It is ridiculous to order an eclogue from a poet as one orders a muslin frock from the dressmakers. . . .

And this is how the thing should be done: the poet must not be expected to deliver his stuff " less than three months after it has been commissioned." But of subjects which truly interested Napoleon he had a better appreciation; thus about history:

> . . . an historian . . . must possess so many qualities, and so many perfections, that it is difficult to believe that good history can ever be produced to order.

And again:

> . . . the art of war as a whole cannot be
> expounded, because it has never yet been
> put on paper — if, indeed, it ever will be.

Nor can the art of governing; but on both it is
worth gathering the *dicta sapientium*, and of these
there are a good many in Napoleon's correspondence. Here are a few examples:

> It is only a step from victory to disaster.
> My experience is that, in a crisis, some de-
> tail always decides the issue. (October 7,
> 1797.)
> Show respect for the nation you govern,
> and show it all the more as you discover less
> grounds for it. (June 5, 1805.)
> Nations cannot be governed by weak-
> ness; it only does them harm. . . . Did
> you really expect to manage people without
> making yourself unpopular? (August 11,
> 1805.)
> I govern by system and not by con-
> cessions. (April 4, 1807.)
> What does the art of governing consist
> in, whether for sovereigns or Ministers? It
> consists in advertising anything well done.
> (April 19, 1807.)

Naturally where military operations were concerned Napoleon's statements of fact were nothing

but verbal manœuvres; and veracity as such did
not enter within his purview. But again his lies
are intellectually tolerable so long as they are good.
Occasionally, however, he oversteps the limits both
of taste and sense — thus in a letter to the Minister
for Foreign Affairs on August 12, 1812:

> We have captured Smolensk without
> the loss of a man. It is a very big town, with
> walls and pretty good fortifications. We
> killed 3 or 4000 of the enemy, wounded
> thrice as many, and found plenty of guns
> here.

What would not a brother or general of Napoleon
have been made to bear for telling a lie so patently
unbelievable! Mr. Thompson states in an editorial
note that "actually the French lost 8–9000 to the
Russians 6000."

This collection of some three hundred letters,
chosen from among 41,000, serves a most valuable purpose as a complement and corrective to
Napoleonic history and biographies. It takes the
reader into the workshop, with all its grime
and noise, and shows how great things were
achieved by genius coupled with limitations
and a certain coarseness. Still, the reader must
remember that the weaker and worse sides of
Napoleon's nature appear more strongly in these
letters; and from that point of view it is good

that those written under the darkening clouds of defeat should come last. Though they are often bitter, and sometimes atrocious in the orders they give, adversity had a humanising effect on Napoleon, as it has on ever so many smaller men.

"MY HEALTH IS GOOD, MY
AFFAIRS ARE GOING WELL"[1]

("Manchester Guardian," May 16, 1935)

THE first long absence of Napoleon from Marie Louise occurred during the Russian campaign of 1812; some ninety letters cover its six months — that is, there are about fifteen to a month — most of them impersonal, empty letters, from a self-centred man absorbed in his work. He cares for the woman who has her place in his world scheme, the daughter of emperors, the mother of " the little King " (thus Napoleon almost invariably refers to his son, aged one). Where advice has to be given it is attentive, clear, and detailed, like his army orders or decrees, but there is never any intimate talk between the two. The disparity is probably too great, the personal element in him seems lost; in the immensity of action he has forfeited his human existence. Words of endearment, significantly, appear as a rule in the language of his early youth: " mio dolce amore," " mio bene." Many a letter reads

[1] " The Letters of Napoleon to Marie Louise," edited by Charles de la Roncière.

185

as if the writer was at a loss how to fill the
sheet of paper; so little has he to tell her about
himself that even short letters are often padded
with speculations about her — where she is, what
she is doing, what she has experienced. Besides,
there are weather reports to fall back upon: dust,
excessive heat, rain, a beautiful autumn, and in the
end the cold, the intolerable cold. These bulletins,
trite and awkward in themselves, become gruesome as they pipe the man and his army to their
doom. And then there enters into that unconscious dirge a stereotyped phrase, which appears
first in a letter from Kovno, on June 26, 1812:
" My health is good, my affairs are going well."
Indifferent to begin with and devoid of contents,
it becomes fixed while the campaign is moving
towards its crisis — a painted smile, a mask, which
in its incongruity gives an ironic, lugubrious, and,
finally, a frantic turn to the scene. On September
3 Napoleon writes from Gat:

> . . . I am leaving to-night to advance
> in the direction of Moscow. We are in
> autumn here. . . . The granaries are full,
> the earth is covered with vegetables; con-
> sequently the troops are well, which is a great
> point. My affairs are going well. My
> health is good. . . .

Now he has repeated the phrase for the thirtieth

time. On September 14 Napoleon reaches Moscow, and on the 16th the city and his plans vanish
in a sea of flames. The phrase is forgotten; it
recurs in two letters of September 20, but fades
out again during the fatal weeks of hesitation at
Moscow. " My health is good " (and nothing
about his affairs) this is the formula used in seven
letters between September 21 and October 4.
And then, in one of the last letters from Moscow:

> Write to your father frequently. Send
> him special couriers; advise him to reinforce
> Schwarzenberg's Corps, so that it may be a
> credit to him.

Napoleon begins to talk business to his big
doll in Paris, and seeks to secure help through her;
the thing is unpleasant, almost painful. The
retreat has started, and the formula about his
health and affairs reappears, but only four times,
last on November 3. On October 26 Napoleon
writes, " I share your desire to see the end of all
this "; and on November 20, " I am in good
health and drawing nearer to you." Now he has
reached the Beresina.

> November 24: The weather is cold.
> . . . My health is very good.
> November 26: My health is very good,
> the cold is very great.

November 28: My health is perfect, the weather very bad and very cold.

December 1: The weather is very cold, my health is very good.

And here, in the last letter from Russia, dated December 5:

You will have seen in the Army Orders that things have [not?] gone as well as I would have wished, yet affairs are not going badly just now. . . . Live in hope and do not worry.

What does the omission of the " not " signify? Usually mistakes of this kind disclose the truth which the writer meant to hide. Napoleon for once intended to tell the truth and finished with a lie.

Another six months, from April to November 1813 — Napoleon's last campaign in Germany — more than a hundred letters. The old formula reappears and is repeated twenty-two times in five months, up to the Battle of Leipzig. But Marie Louise is constantly urged to write to " Papa François," to inform him, to plead with him. Austria holds the key to the European position.

May 2: Write and tell Papa François not to allow himself to be led away by the hatred his wife bears us, that it would be fatal to himself and the source of many calamities. . . .

May 5: Papa François is not behaving himself very well. . . .

May 14: People are trying to mislead Papa François. Metternich is a mere intriguer.

June 27: I want peace, but it must be an honourable one.

July 7: If they attempt to impose shameful terms upon me, I will make war upon them. Austria will pay for it all.

August 17: Deceived by Metternich, your father has sided with my enemies.

August 18: Do not worry too much about your father's conduct.

In this second stage, while Napoleon is trying to work through Marie Louise, the correspondence gains in contents and acquires something of a human touch.

And next: 1814. The Empire has disappeared, France is invaded, the faith and awe which surrounded Napoleon's person are gone — a dead scene with a cold aftermath. A fortnight before the final catastrophe, on March 17, 1814, Napoleon writes from Rheims to Marie Louise:

MA BONNE LOUISE,—I have received your letter. I hope the weather in Paris is

189

as fine as it is in Rheims. It will be very
convenient for your outings and will do good
for your health. Give a kiss to the King and
never doubt the love I bear you.

Ton
NAP.

When the end has come he appeals to the
woman, his wife, the mother of his son, to join
him. The doll hesitates for a moment, and then
there is no reply.

" LA DÉGRINGOLADE "[1]

(" *Manchester Guardian*," *September* 30, 1938)

THE story of March and April 1814, of Napoleon's defeat and abdication, can be summed up in the word " la dégringolade," which in colloquial English means " how everything went to pieces." It is a depressing story in which no one is at his best; the narrative meanders in an atmosphere of supreme malaise; nothing is great or impressive, not even the so-called betrayal and desertion of Napoleon by his Marshals and Ministers. Tired men fumble about and slither on ground on which they cannot stand or walk. In the closing stages of history's greatest epic they have but one wish: that it were all over. Selfishness, cowardice, and resentments had their share, but they were not the determining factor. Napoleon claimed that had he not been betrayed and abandoned he could yet have won; but could any enlightened Frenchman wish him to win? The only result would have been further wars and a prolonged agony which some time, somewhere, was bound to find its

[1] " Memoirs of General de Caulaincourt, Duke of Vicenza," vol. ii., 1814, edited by Jean Hanoteau.

disastrous term. There are circumstances in which even defeatism has its excuse.

By 1814 France, no less than the rest of Europe, had realized that a durable peace was not possible with and under Napoleon; further, that he was neither invincible nor infallible. He had started blundering even in matters of strategy, and blunders, like crimes, produce offspring at the rate of insects. Something had gone wrong; something had slipped from him; strike a wrong key and you get out of touch with your machine; he had lost the grip of things. The man who in the past was able to gauge others, forestall them, lead them, or force them into his own ways, and who, above all men, knew the value of time, now began to lag behind events rather than meet and master them. At Prague, at Frankfort, and at Chatillon he had a chance of securing a respite. He knew that he needed it; otherwise he would not have entered into negotiations while the tide was running against him and his opponents could stake out their claims in terms of an anticipated future. But no sooner did he perceive, or think he perceived, a glimmer of hope than he would go back on the instructions and powers which he had given to his plenipotentiaries. Even when the time had come for unconditional abdication, he still tried to prevaricate, forgetting that ambiguity, like moral indignation and rudeness, is the privilege

of the stronger. Napoleon only recovered his
intellectual greatness when he abandoned hope;
till then he was self-conscious and preoccupied,
given over to self-deception and to accusing others.
What he said at that time about the French, was
true of himself: " They are unhappy, and the
unhappy are unjust." But when at last he gave
up the game for lost, before his attempted suicide
and after, he once more came to view men and
matters with impersonal objectivity; and the talks
which he had in those days with Caulaincourt
form the most interesting chapter in this volume.

Accurate evaluation correlated to a purpose
was Napoleon's normal approach to human beings.
He assessed but did not value them; was lavish
in rewards and chary of praise; disparaging, but
not prone to blame and still less to punish. He
was a hard taskmaster, exhausting and discourag-
ing; altogether inhuman. And, in turn, men with
whom he was in closer contact had little human
feeling for him. So long as he was victorious, they
followed him in mute admiration. He thought,
spoke, and acted for all. Only when he began to
totter France regained voice and action; and the
long-suppressed protest, fanned by patriotic fears,
broke out in betrayal and desertion. Marshal
Ney, Prince de la Moskowa, who a year later was
to rejoin Napoleon and suffer execution for it,
when sent by him to the headquarters of the Allies

in Paris, in the presence of the Tsar indulged in indiscreet and injudicious criticisms of Napoleon; but then it was new to him to be able to speak his mind.

Caulaincourt remained at the very end correctly loyal and consciously correct. But there is something strained about his attitude, a degree of self-congratulation on having " pulled it off," which, combined with an almost envious reprehension of the others, shows how much it must have cost him not to follow their example. Even he did not love Napoleon, and Napoleon knew it; nor could he have contemplated new Napoleonic victories without apprehension. He merely wished the Emperor to secure a reasonable existence within reasonable frontiers; which, seeing the nature and ante-cedents of the man, was not a reasonable wish. It might even be asked whether Caulaincourt's more enduring attachment to Napoleon was not per-haps, at least subconsciously, connected with the part, mistakenly but widely, ascribed to Caulain-court in the capture and execution of the Duc d'Enghien.

THE BRAYING OF A JACKASS [1]

(" *Manchester Guardian*," *December* 6, 1932)

GENIUS is capacity for great constructive achievement, but it does not exempt from blunders or weakness. How else could Napoleon have let General Gourgaud be one of the few companions allowed to him at St. Helena? It is enough to look at the man's picture, his garrulous, wide-open eyes, at his blabbing, argumentative mouth, at his forehead of a half-wit, at the excitable stupidity of his face, to see what Napoleon let himself in for; it " portrays a man who would have tried the patience of Job." But then Napoleon had not chosen him. " I have often heard the Emperor say to the Empress Josephine," writes Gourgaud, " that he yields to one thing only — importunity." Gourgaud was at Rochefort; when he heard that he was to be left behind he made a violent scene. Napoleon gave in; and Gourgaud continued making scenes.

He was jealous, touchy, egotistical, and always

---

[1] " The St. Helena Journal of General Baron Gourgaud, 1815–1818," translated by Sydney Gillard and edited by Norman Edwards.

on his dignity — or his " honour," as he called it. " Honour " had bid him accompany Napoleon into exile (or rather force his company on the Emperor); and after that he claimed to have made a sacrifice of his life, and thought he should be treated accordingly. At every opportunity he recounted what he had done for Napoleon; there was especially one incident he could not forget (nor accurately remember): how once with a pistol-shot he had saved the Emperor's life when an enemy rushed at him; sometimes it was a hussar with a sword, and sometimes a Cossack with a lance. When the wife of one of the other companions of Napoleon expected a child and a room was added for them, Gourgaud wrote: " I couldn't bear to see building being done for the Montholons if something similar was not done for me." Whether he was properly placed in a picture of the party at Long-wood, or how he was mentioned in a letter by Napoleon, was of course of supreme importance to him.

How do you wish me to speak of you? (asked the Emperor). You are always afraid of compromising yourself. I should have to consult you on every occasion to know whether what I say pleases you or not. That's not my custom, and it doesn't suit me.

196

THE BRAYING OF A JACKASS

" I am too richly endowed with affection " is
Gourgaud's own diagnosis of his case.

What is the value of the memoirs of such a
man? In certain ways small, in other ways considerable. Comparatively little appears in this
Journal of Napoleon's personality, but as Gourgaud was too egotistical and too stupid to fall in
with the drama which Napoleon staged at St.
Helena, the braying of the jackass often breaks
in on it in a manner valuable to those who want
to get at the real facts. Moreover, the degrada-
tion of that life in a cage was fully within the
range of Gourgaud's powers to experience and
describe. A Boswell might have overlooked it,
entranced by the Emperor's mind and engrossed
in recording his sayings; or it might have escaped
the observation of a truly devoted companion
trying to make things more tolerable for the
Emperor. But if anyone wants a pitiful, hopeless,
ludicrous picture of the great captive, grappling,
for instance, with the problem of a cow, and
getting angry when things went wrong, here he
can find it.

> The Emperor is in a very bad humour,
> and full of the cow incident. At dinner, the
> Emperor asks Archambault: " Did you let
> the cow get away? If it is lost, you'll pay for
> it, you blackguard! " Archambault assures
> his Majesty that he caught the cow again at

the other end of the park; that she twice
broke her rope, and that she gives no milk.
I hold my tongue throughout the meal. His
Majesty, in a very bad humour, retires at
10.30, muttering: " Moscow! Half a million
men! "

And lastly, that picture of unspeakable boredom:
" I am oppressed with boredom," writes Gour-
gaud.   " Boredom. . . . Great boredom. . . .
Terrible boredom."

" What's the time? " inquired the Emperor.
" Ten o'clock, sire."   " Let's go to bed, then."

NAPOLEON II [1]

("*Manchester Guardian*," March 20, 1933)

THE Emperor died with his eyes fixed in silence
on the portraits and bust of his son. What was
the personality of that boy on whom the title of
" King of Rome " was bestowed in his cradle, to
whom a World Empire was to have descended as
inheritance, and who, in turn, by his birth had
seemed to add to the stability and duration of that
Empire? Chateaubriand said about the son of
the Corsican and the Austrian archduchess that
" his mother gave him the past, his father the
future "; but " the future " was dead before
the boy could understand its meaning, and " the
past " became for him a golden cage. " My birth
and my death — that is my whole story," said
Napoleon's son on his death-bed.

In 1814 he was separated from his father, who
adored him, and soon after deserted by his mother;
he was brought up by his grandfather, the Emperor
Francis I of Austria, who loved him in a human
way but left the making, or rather the unmaking,
of his life to Metternich. And in that child

---

[1] " Napoleon II, the King of Rome," by Octave Aubry.

Metternich still waged war on the shadow and memory of the man whom he had feared, loathed, cajoled, fought, and vanquished in the great battle of his life. The boy was deprived of his royal title, even of his name; he was no longer King of Rome, nor Napoleon, nor a Frenchman, but " Francis," a Habsburg, an Austrian prince, Duke of Reichstadt. The name and memory of the father, which with ever-growing force resounded throughout the world in posthumous conquest, were to be extinguished from the consciousness of his son. None the less, as he grew up the legend reached him, and the tragedy of his life began, to be cut short by death from consumption at the age of twenty-one.

Metternich now wrote to the Austrian Ambassador in Paris asking him to call Louis-Philippe's attention " to the person who will succeed the Duke."

> I use the word " succeed," for in the Bonapartist hierarchy there is a succession openly avowed and respected by the party. Young Louis Bonaparte is deeply involved in intrigues of faction; he was never placed, like the Duke of Reichstadt, under the safeguard of the Emperor's principles.

And the Emperor Francis, according to M. Aubry,

> mourned the innocent child, the delightful

youth who had been his favourite. But he could not help regarding his death as a deliverance. He was beyond suffering, and he had ceased to be a political embarrassment. The grandfather . . . had been neither willing nor able to achieve the boy's happiness. He was glad to shoulder off the responsibility upon God.

TALLEYRAND

(" *Manchester Guardian,*" *May* 17, 1938)

Talleyrand was born in 1754, fifteen years
before Napoleon, and died on May 17, 1838,
surviving him by another seventeen years. He
collaborated with Mirabeau and Sieyès in 1789,
and with Guizot and Thiers under the July
Monarchy. Of high aristocracy, he entered the
Church because lameness, due to an accident in
childhood, precluded army service. As Bishop of
Autun he was returned by the clergy to the States-
General, had a share in drafting the Declaration
of the Rights of Man, and played a leading part
in the Constituent Assembly. In October 1789
he moved the appropriation of the Church property
by the State, and on July 14, 1790, at the feast on
the Champ de Mars commemorating the Bastille,
in the presence of Louis XVI, he celebrated the
Mass ("Pray, don't make me laugh," he whispered
to Lafayette). Early in 1791 he discarded the
vestments which had never meant anything to him.
When, six years later, his appointment to the
Foreign Office was discussed in the Directory
Carnot objected : he would sell them all. " Whom
has he sold? " replied La Revellière. " First, his

God." " He was never a believer." " . . . Next,
his order." " A mark of philosophy." " Rather
of ambition. Lastly, his King." " It is hardly for
us to reproach him with that."

Talleyrand had no moral principles or scruples,
few illusions or dreams. He was the least romantic
of men. Metternich was a romantic with regard
to his doctrines; Talleyrand had no doctrines.
He had a strong sense of reality and clear judgment. He appreciated spiritual values, but in a
curiously detached manner. He was lazy, and
boasted of it. Neglected by his parents in early
childhood and brought up by dependents, he was
a *grand seigneur* towards men of other classes but
had no love for his own and contributed with cold
indifference to its downfall. He had few deeper
human contacts and knew neither gratitude nor
personal loyalty. He had self-love but little self-
respect, no love or respect for others. The world
of the *ancien régime* had its standards of honour, its
conventions and barriers (though few sincere pre-
judices); these aids to morality, or substitutes for
it, had been swept away. Talleyrand, emotionally
detached and spiritually free, worked in a moral
and social void. He loved women and money;
he cared for France. There was hardly a limit to
which he would not demean himself for the sake
of money; he took colossal bribes for treaties and
frontiers — the jackal of Napoleon's campaigns.

This craving was pathological and in a way pathetic; to him money stood for concrete security in a world full of dangers and unreality. Foremost, he meant to live.

Survival, free of the stigma of emigration, was his aim under the Terror. " I placed myself at the disposal of events, and, provided I remained a Frenchman, I would put up with anything." After August 10, 1792, he wrote an exculpating diplomatic circular, but for himself secured a pass-port from Danton: " Laissez passer, &c. Maurice Talleyrand, allant à Londres par nos ordres." He remained in this country till expelled in 1794. He then proceeded to the United States, where he tried his hand at land speculation (he was even scheming to make Hindu gentlemen invest in American real estate). He was allowed to return to France in 1796. In July 1797 he was given the Foreign Office — a subordinate post, as policy was made by the Directory. On his way to thank Barras he muttered rapturously that now he would amass " une fortune immense, une immense fortune, une immense fortune, une fortune immense." The Americans were shocked when, to obtain justice from one they had so lately befriended, they had to bribe him with £50,000. By 1799 he had 3,000,000 francs on deposit with Hamburg and London banks; in 1805 his fortune was valued at 40,000,000.

M. Lacour-Gayet in his great work on Talleyrand paints his first meeting with Bonaparte.
Tall, with his hair powdered as under the *ancien
régime*, high cheek-bones, round chin, his eyes
fixed, his pointed nose insolently raised, his lips
curved in irony and disdain, a very high stock
round his neck, stiff and immobile to disguise his
limp, he bore an air of fatigue and supreme in-
difference which made him look older than forty-
three. The other man, small and thin, with quick,
nervous movements, olive skin, long black hair,
severe countenance, sharp nose, tight lips, protrud-
ing chin, already conveyed an impression of
irresistible force; he had conquered Italy, was
about to attack England, wore the uniform of
commander-in-chief, and was twenty-eight. " Il y
a là de l'avenir" was Talleyrand's comment on
Bonaparte. In November 1792 Talleyrand had
argued the uselessness of conquests, " France
should remain within her own frontiers " — she
owes this to herself and to others. In July 1798:
" The Republic inspires respect rather than confidence; through confidence alone is it possible to
gain true and useful allies." In 1800 he foresaw
that further conquests would prove " a career
without term." He preached moderation; he
was to serve Napoleon. " He signed events but
did not make them."

Talleyrand now professed unbounded admira-

tion for Napoleon. Napoleon appreciated Talleyrand: " He has great advantages as a negotiator
. . . he knows the foreign courts, has finesse . . .
an utterly impassive face, and a great name. To
the Revolution he belongs only by his miscon-
duct. . . ." Yet it was not an easy partnership
between the cultured and lazy aristocrat and the
man who worked like no one else and was " in-
amusable." The Napoleonic Empire was fast
becoming a danger to France, and after Eylau
Talleyrand said to Prince Dalberg that had
Napoleon been killed they would have made
Joseph his successor, but proclaimed " an immediate and absolute withdrawal of France to her
Rhine frontier."

Gradually his misgivings thickened, and he
resigned the Foreign Office in August 1807. Still
he remained at Court, and in 1808, a secret
enemy, accompanied Napoleon to the famous
interview with Tsar Alexander at Erfurt. " The
French people is civilised, but not its sovereign,"
he said to Alexander; " Russia's sovereign is
civilised, but not its people; the Russian sovereign
should therefore be the ally of the French people."
And again: " The Rhine, the Alps, and the
Pyrenees are the conquests of France; the rest, of
the Emperor; they mean nothing to France." An
entente was established between the two against
Napoleon.

When news about Talleyrand's activities and Austria's intrigues reached Napoleon, he suddenly returned to his capital, and on January 28, 1809, received Talleyrand in the presence of several Court officials and Ministers. For half an hour he poured out a torrent of the most violent abuse against Talleyrand, concluding with a coarse reference to his wife. When leaving Talleyrand remarked, " What a pity that so great a man should be so ill-bred! "

In 1812, and again in 1813, Napoleon offered the Foreign Office to Talleyrand. He refused. On March 31, 1814, came the hour of his vengeance and of his greatest achievement. This was one of those rare occasions when an idea can shape the fate of nations. The Allies were about to enter Paris; the future of France was dark. Talleyrand saw the road to salvation: the Bourbons had to be restored. They had been forgotten; they were strangers to modern France, but Europe needed them. What Europe had fought, and still feared, was the French Revolution and Napoleon. The Bourbons were a natural barrier against both, acceptable, or at least tolerable, to France. Napoleon was Emperor of the French, successor to Caesar and Charlemagne; they were Kings of France, heirs to Louis XIV. With the Bourbons France could resume *les anciennes limites*. But the sins of the Revolution and Napoleon must not be visited on Bourbon France. Had not the Bourbons been the first sufferers and victims? The greatest transformation trick of history was played. France was absolved of guilt and escaped punishment. When in 1918–19 the German Republic tried to repeat the trick it did not work; some of those who had fought " to make the world safe for democracy " now feared Bolshevism more than the Kaiser.

It was not mere cynicism in Talleyrand to come forward as the apostle of *légitimité*. A tired, ageing man, he tried to gather up broken threads. At the Congress of Vienna he worked with the pacific and conservative Powers, Great Britain and Austria. Europe was not to be remodelled when France could not profit by it. This opposition to Russia counted against Talleyrand when, after Waterloo, France required her protection. A few months later he retired into private life.

He emerged once more after the July Revolution. Victorious, France tries to establish her own system on the Continent; defeated, or in times of weakness, she turns to England or Russia, the choice being largely determined by conditions at home. In 1830 help had to be sought in London, and Talleyrand became the maker of the first Franco-British Entente, in defence of French liberalism and of the Belgian revolution. He established close co-operation with British statesmen.

" We have to deal here with timid people," he wrote. " Ils arrivent un peu lentement, mais enfin ils arrivent."

Talleyrand on his death-bed accepted the rites of the Church, but he remembered the privilege of his pre-Revolution state. He received the holy oil with his hands closed and his palms turned downwards, murmuring, " Do not forget I am a bishop."

MEN WHO FLOUNDERED
INTO THE WAR

PRINCE VON BÜLOW

I [1]

("*Observer*," May 31, 1931)

The German editor of Prince Bülow's "Memoirs" writes in his preface:

Prince Bülow devoted five years to dictating his "Memoirs," and three further years to the careful, laborious revision of the text. . . . There was not a name, not a date, not a quotation, that was not verified repeatedly by the use of reference books. There was not a sentence that was not carefully weighed and pondered again and again. The growth of the work was considerably facilitated by the Prince's unusually powerful memory . . . a memory that hoarded not only historical persons and events, but significant quotations. . . . Of documents in the strict sense of the word there were very little. There were in particular few letters.

---

[1] "Memoirs, 1897–1903," vol. i., by Prince von Bülow Translated by F. A. Voigt.

The dire meaning of this passage gradually dawns on the reader as he ploughs through the 620 large pages of the first volume. It contains little original material; either Prince Bülow failed to preserve it, or the choice he made for reproduction was singularly poor. Congratulatory messages from august personages and letters of adulation from subordinates take up at least as much space as historical documents; and the Prince's "unusually powerful memory" fills the book with masses of insipid anecdote, of irrelevant information, and of tiresome literary quotations — the narrative stagnates, while the smooth *causeur* chatters.

> Even when I was at school I had a taste, or a weakness, for quotations. When an idea came into my head I preferred to leave it in the form which some great prose writer or poet had discovered before me.

Thought is thus suffocated by vain erudition, which, moreover, incessantly indulges in stuff like this — presumably "verified by the use of reference books":

> The Cyclades and Sporades were settled by Ionians, the Thracian Islands successively by Athens and Sparta, Macedonia and Rome, Byzantium and Venice, and finally by the Osmans, and now a German ship was carrying the German Emperor past them to

the former residence of the Emperor Con-
stantine and Sultan Soliman.

The book might well have been written by an
elderly lady-in-waiting, originally chosen for her
looks, noble birth, social polish, and liberal education, qualities in which she herself took considerable pride; being observant, she picked up a
certain amount of information, which, when carefully collated with more authoritative materials,
may prove of some historical value; and having
been dismissed from Court, she takes her cattish
revenge by ridiculing her late masters and reviling
her successors. But here the author is a statesman
who for twelve years controlled the policy of
Imperial Germany, first as Secretary of State, and
next as Chancellor! Something of this incredible
production may be ascribed to senility, but most
of it undoubtedly reflects the man's normal self.
He had seemed important when in charge of one
of the most powerful political machines ever constructed — but then how great, nay, superhuman,
some one switching on electric light would appear
to a Martian who had never seen it done, and
knew nothing about the mechanism. People may
sententiously repeat the saying about the little
wisdom with which the world is ruled — they do
not really believe it, and, in the absence of personal
experience, can hardly conceive it.

Of political thought and penetration, of a
critical analysis or evaluation of events there is
nothing in this fat volume; nor is there a trace of
real wit, amusing malice, or finesse. It is all so
crude, flat, and childish — an unconscious, pitiless
exposure of a pitiful set which ruled and ruined a
nation, hard-working and intelligent, even though
uncouth and, in a deeper sense, not altogether
civilized. The insincerity of the author is trans-
parent, and even more unpleasant than his un-
ceasing attacks on William II are his attempts
at camouflaging them. Here is his account of
a cruise with the Emperor:

> The weather was beautiful; the Baltic
> as calm as an inland lake, which was just
> what the Kaiser wanted. He was filled with
> a passionate love for the sea, but, like his
> mother, the Empress Frederick, and also like
> Admiral Nelson, he was plagued with sea-
> sickness.

Yes, exactly like Nelson; and then:

> . . . every naval officer would tell me
> that no one knew the naval signals better
> than the Kaiser, that no one knew the tech-
> nical vocabulary of navigation so well as he,
> yet that he was quite incapable of sailing the
> tiniest vessel. . . .

> William II loved display; he used . . .

216

to wear as many orders as he could. His self-esteem rose when he took a field-marshal's baton in his hand, or, on shipboard, the admiral's telescope, which, on the high seas, replaces the marshal's baton.

Although in appearance Bülow defends the Kaiser against the accusation of cowardice, he does his best to cover the All-Highest War Lord with ridicule. Here are a few examples. William II was fond of giving away a picture in which he appeared " with sword uplifted, leading his Royal Uhlans in a manœuvre attack."

This picture showed what he really wanted: a smart " conduct " and a " dashing " manner, but no real danger, no serious test. He never wanted to ride in any attacks but those made in manœuvres.

These attacks were specially prepared for His Majesty. The ground was chosen months beforehand and put in order. The royal horses were taken over it till they knew it perfectly. As far as human calculation could foresee everything would go well.

What William II most desired . . . was to see himself, at the head of a glorious German Fleet, starting out on a peaceful visit to England. The English Sovereign, with his fleet, would meet the German Kaiser in Portsmouth. The two fleets would file past each other, the two Monarchs, each wearing the naval uniform of the other's country, and wearing the other's decorations, would then stand on the bridges of their flagships. Then, after they had embraced in the prescribed manner, a gala dinner with lovely speeches would be held in Cowes.

. . . this same Monarch, who . . . never had his fill of parades and parade marches, cavalry charges, and frontal attacks on the manœuvre ground, drew back when Bellona turned her stern face towards him and real war began.

. . . a Prussian king who, in that moment, could do no more than apply his proved capacities to standing for hours at one spot in ignorance of all that was passing and in complete passivity, impresses one as a mockery of all Prussia's history.

Nor does Bülow, in a book which deals with the years 1897–1903, miss a chance of referring to the " painful " subject of the Emperor's flight to Holland in 1918.

Bülow finds it easy to make fun of the Kaiser's " unquenchable flood of eloquence," of the un-easiness felt by other sovereigns when exposed to his oratory, of the way in which after every speech his entourage and Ministers had to try to prevent its being published as delivered. There are hints throughout the book that mentally the Kaiser was

not altogether normal, but the suggestion is always
ascribed to others, and loyally, or charitably,
denied by Bülow. In 1897 Count Monts reported
from Munich " great joy . . . over the exalted
orator . . . who is clearly no longer a responsible
person," and the Chancellor, Prince Hohenlohe,
anxiously inquired of Bülow whether he " considered that the Kaiser was really absolutely sane."
At Jerusalem, when the Kaiser was about to deliver a speech in church, the Empress herself is
described as casting " anxious looks " at Bülow.

> She was evidently seized with fear lest
> her consort, overpowered by the solemnity
> of the moment and under the influence of
> the frightful heat, might no longer be quite
> in his right mind.

In 1900 Prince Philip Eulenburg, considered
an intimate friend of the Kaiser's, feared " a
nervous crisis the character of which cannot be
foretold," and in 1903, during a cruise " on
board this floating theatre " (the Imperial yacht),
the Emperor " made a terrible impression " on
him — " pale, glancing about him uneasily, orat-
ing, and piling lie upon lie. Not healthy — this is
probably the mildest verdict that can be given."
But Bülow defends his late friend and master:

> I feel bound to reiterate once more that
> I am firmly convinced that William II was

219

not mentally deficient, but he was certainly superficial, hypersensitive to impressions, lacking in self-criticism and self-control. . . .

The years of 1898–1901 were crucial in the history of Anglo-German relations. These were the years of Mr. Joseph Chamberlain's plans for a close understanding or alliance, of the agreements concerning Samoa and the Portuguese colonies, of England's search for a new orientation, "splendid isolation" being no longer practicable. Bülow in his "Memoirs" refrains from going systematically through the history of these talks and negotiations, nor does he explain his own, now published, despatches on the subject. But it is clear that he did not expect this country to reach an understanding with France and Russia, that he suspected British statesmen of a design to use Germany as a cat's-paw against them, and that he hoped to get the better of Great Britain by withholding the promise of German support until a critical moment when Great Britain would have to pay for it any price which Germany might demand. Whatever the part of Herr von Holstein and of the Emperor may have been in the rejection of the advances from Great Britain, the final responsibility for it falls on Bülow. He prefers, however, to throw all the blame for subsequent developments on his successors whom

the Homeric scholar never names without an
epitheton ornans — Bethmann Hollweg is always
" wretched and sanctimonious," " clumsy," " ineffective," " awkward and simple," etc., etc.
One wonders to what extent Bülow's description
of other men and their doings is really an unconscious, accurate estimate of his own self. He
writes:

> When I look back upon these intrigues,
> so often petty, still more often spiteful and
> low, I understand everything said by great
> poets, from Sophocles to Shakespeare, and
> deep thinkers, from La Rochefoucauld and
> Montaigne to Schopenhauer, about the low
> instincts of mankind and the worthlessness
> of the world. Though here I must not forget
> to add that I believe things to be no better
> in other countries. . . . The reason of such
> occurrences lies as little in the form of
> government as in the climate or in the race;
> it is to be found in the baseness of human
> nature itself.

II [1]

(" Week-end Review," January 9, 1932)

The second volume of Bülow's " Memoirs " is
superior to the first. Some important documents

[1] " Memoirs, 1903–1909," vol. ii., by Prince von Bülow.
Translated by Geoffrey Dunlop and F. A. Voigt.

are reproduced, and certain crucial transactions of his Chancellorship elucidated, while the worst tricks of the author seem to have been, to some extent, worked off in the first volume; there are fewer literary tags and quotations, fewer irrelevant stories, and there is less of his " loving " abuse of William II.

Not that those tricks are dropped altogether. The Emperor, a " gifted, nobly-endowed character," is shown sending the Tsar pictures by his favourite painter, Knackfuss, " as his own works," or publishing under his own name Prince Eulenburg's song " Aegir." He was " so lovable and so amiable, so natural and so simple, so large-hearted and so broad-minded " — " I loved him with my whole heart." This does not prevent Bülow from gloating over his flight to Holland; from sneering at the " Admiral of the Atlantic " who was unable to steer a yacht without bumping into something, and at the Supreme War-Lord who delighted in showy parades, but feared war; and from describing him altogether as a coward, a braggart, and a liar. One such lie Bülow — characteristically — reported to Dr. Renvers, against whom it was directed, asking for a medical explanation of the case.

Renvers . . . answered: " If the Emperor were an ordinary patient I should

222

diagnose *Pseudologia phantastica*." When I
asked him to explain this technical term, he
said with a laugh: " A tendency to live in
phantasy. Or, to put it quite bluntly, to lie."

But while scathingly critical of the Kaiser,
Bülow seems unwittingly to emulate him in his
conceit as orator, statesman, soldier on parade, and
God's own chosen instrument. Here are a few
examples:

> . . . the value of words is incalculable. I
> doubt whether, in 1906, we should have won
> such brilliant victories over Socialism if my
> Reichstag speeches of the previous months
> had not been circulated in millions of copies,
> and paved the way for our victory.

In a letter to the Minister for War, on July 1,
1906:

> God's help has enabled me to guide
> Germany safely through the danger in
> Morocco. . . .

To the Emperor, in November 1908, on the effect
of some of his telegrams and speeches:

> The . . . distrust . . . evoked in all
> parties and classes of the nation, though it
> in no way shakes my confidence in God, in
> Your Majesty, and in Germany, compels me
> to use prudent tactics . . .

On a circular which Bülow had written and
" brought to the direct notice of the Emperor
Francis Joseph ":

> His Apostolic Majesty . . . certainly
> owed to it his power of resistance to the
> blandishments of the tempter Edward VII,
> whom he withstood on 13th August at Ischl
> far more successfully than did our mother
> Eve the serpent.

And here is Bülow at the Imperial manœuvres
of 1905:

> To my joy, in the course of these
> manœuvres, the Kaiser permitted me twice
> to lead my old regiment past the flag — at
> the trot and the gallop. When after the
> march past I pulled up left of His Majesty
> with the regulation volt, Deines, who stood
> next the Kaiser, said to me: " Your beautiful
> volt gives the Kaiser far greater pleasure
> than the longest memorandum you could
> draw up for him." Later I greeted the officers
> of my regiment, many of whom, within ten
> years, were to seal with their blood their
> loyalty to King and Country. . . . At the
> end of these manœuvres, immediately after
> the defile, the Emperor handed me my brevet
> as General à la suite, with uniform of the
> Royal Hussars. Here is the text. . . .

These " Memoirs " are an incredible exposure,

not of the Kaiser and of Bülow alone, but of Germany's pre-war policy. Were any justification required for Great Britain's attitude towards Germany during the years 1903–1909, none better could be found than in this volume. The exotic schemings of the Emperor, his offer of the old Kingdom of Burgundy to the King of the Belgians, his plan to force Denmark into a political surrender to Germany, the German calculations how much longer they would have to mind their conduct towards Great Britain (*i.e.* how soon their fleet would enable them to assume a different tone), and, finally, the prospect of such an instrument in the hands of a man whom Bülow himself describes as irresponsible and downright psychopathic — who, in view of these facts frankly admitted by the ex-Chancellor, can say that either our suspicions or our caution were unfounded? To the Germans, and especially to William II, the most innocent suggestion of an agreement for the limitation of naval armaments was an indignity touching their " national honour " — the Emperor " was set against all and every attempt at a naval understanding with England." Meantime British statesmen quietly ignored German provocations and blunders. Thus Bülow himself writes after the Emperor's interview with the " Daily Telegraph ": " I am bound to admit that, officially, the English remained correct and friendly."

One of the most interesting chapters in the book is that on the " Daily Telegraph " interview; and from that, when the story is told in full, the Emperor comes out better than Bülow. The interview was written up, in the autumn of 1908, by an English friend of the Emperor's from political pronouncements which the Emperor had made in private company, almost a year earlier, during his visit to England, and it was sent to him for approval. The Emperor, very correctly, submitted it to Bülow, who, instead of examining it himself, handed it on to some subordinates. These did not dare to raise objections to anything which came from the Emperor, and returned the paper without criticism to Bülow, who released it without ever having read it. None the less he seems to have felt nothing more than a formal responsibility in the matter, and if hereafter he defended the Emperor, in however slighting a manner, he thought this heroic loyalty on his own part, for which he made the Emperor submit to numerous lectures on his behaviour.

CONRAD VON HÖTZENDORF

I

1852–1914

(" *Manchester Guardian*," *August* 27, 1925)

FIELD-MARSHAL FRANCIS CONRAD VON HÖTZEN-
DORF was born at Penzing, near Vienna, in 1852;
he was educated at the Military Academy at
Wiener-Neustadt, and as a lieutenant served in
the Bosnian campaign of 1878. Subsequently, as
a teacher at a military school, he wrote a book
on infantry tactics which became a manual in the
Austro-Hungarian army. In 1906 he was appointed Chief of the General Staff.

From the very outset he championed an
aggressive policy, and hardly anyone in Europe
in a responsible position during those fatal years
had an equal record of constant incitement to
war. In 1907 he pressed for war against Italy,
in January 1908 he declared that " the problem
of Serbia and Montenegro should be solved during the coming year by war; we could also deal
simultaneously with Italy." In 1909 he advo-

227

cated the annexation of Serbia, and the fact that
the Bosnian crisis passed without war and conquest left him with a rankling grievance on which
he constantly harped. When in 1911 Italy had
engaged on the Tripolitan expedition, Conrad
demanded that advantage should be taken of her
temporary weakness. Venetia should be annexed.
Such a war, he argued, would raise the spirit of
the Austro-Hungarian army, which " has suffered
from the policy of continuous compromise, hesitations, and concessions." In the memorandum
to the Emperor dated November 15, 1911, he
demanded war against Italy for the spring of
1912. Count Aehrental, though mortally ill,
with all his waning strength opposed Conrad's
policy of aggression. The Emperor Francis
Joseph took Aehrental's side, and very sharply
reprimanded Conrad for " the continuous attacks
against Aehrental," declaring the peace policy to
be his own and telling Conrad that " everybody
had to accommodate himself to it "; however
probable the war with Italy might be, it should
not come unless Italy provoked it. The Emperor
closed the talk with the pointed remark that " up
to now there never has been a war party in our
midst." Conrad drew the consequences, and his
resignation was immediately accepted. On November 30, 1911, he was appointed Army Inspector.

In 1912 followed the Balkan wars, and on

December 6 Conrad, who at that time had a warm supporter in the heir apparent, the Archduke Francis Ferdinand, was re-appointed Chief of the General Staff. He now felt that he had come into his own, and with increased zest resumed his war propaganda. In January 1913, he officially demanded a general mobilization against Serbia to be declared on March 1 and to be followed by war. He failed once more, as Germany refused to let herself be dragged into war, and even the Archduke Francis Ferdinand was opposed to it. Another " chance " was missed to Conrad's intense grief.

II

JUNE–AUGUST 1914 [1]

(" The Times," December 13, 1923)

WHEN the news of the Sarajevo murder reached Field-Marshal Conrad von Hötzendorf, he, for one, felt no need to inquire whether any responsibility for it rested with Serbia, or to make up his mind as to the course to be taken. On June 29 he told Count Berchtold, the Austro-Hungarian Minister for Foreign Affairs, that immediate action was required, and that it should

[1] Conrad von Hötzendorf, " Aus meiner Dienstzeit," vol. iv.

be a mobilization against Serbia. Berchtold replied that he wished to await the result of the judicial inquiry; and this view, as Berchtold informed Conrad on July 1, was shared by the Emperor and by Count Tisza, the Hungarian, and Count Stuergkh, the Austrian Prime Minister. " Tisza," he said, " was opposed to war against Serbia, as he feared that Russia would attack and Germany desert us. Stuergkh, on the other hand, expected the inquiry to yield good grounds for action. I maintained that an energetic stroke alone could avert the danger from Serbia. The murder committed under her auspices supplied the ground for war."

" Material relating to time previous to murder yields no evidence of propaganda having been supported by the Serbian Government . . ." wired on July 13 from Sarajevo Herr von Wiesner, who had been sent by the Austro-Hungarian Foreign Office to inquire into the matter. " Nothing proves, or even suggests that the Serbian Government had a hand in organizing or preparing the murder or that it supplied the arms." But Conrad treated such evidence as nothing better than " a preliminary account of the point then reached in the inquiry " into a question which he, from the very first, had settled in his mind, without any evidence whatsoever. In fact, his endless, wearisome, hackneyed references to

Serbia's " crime," to her " brutal provocation "
of the Habsburg Monarchy, etc., are nothing but
his habitual, though much-belated, cant.

His real reasons are acknowledged at the
outset of this volume:

" Two principles were in sharp conflict: the
maintenance of Austria as a conglomerate of
various nationalities . . . and the rise of independent national States claiming their ethnic
territories from Austria-Hungary." Serb activities
brought this conflict to a head, and " for this
reason, and not with a view to expiating the
murder, Austria-Hungary had to go to war against
Serbia."

But even in the minds of those who professed
the desire to await the results of the judicial
inquiry (in the firm hope that it could be made
to prove what they desired) the foremost question
was whether, if Austria plunged into war, she
could count on the absolute support of Germany
— during the Balkan wars Germany had refused
to support the war party in Austria. Berchtold's
chef de cabinet, Count Hoyos, was therefore sent
to Berlin — the fatal significance and results of
this mission have recently been fully disclosed by
a late official of the Austro-Hungarian Foreign
Office; the German Emperor was got to commit
himself in his typically impetuous way, and an
understanding was reached with Zimmermann,

the Under-Secretary of the German Foreign
Office, who henceforth co-operated with the most
extreme war party in Austria.

> To-morrow we shall have a reply [said
> Berchtold to Conrad on July 6]. The Ger-
> man Emperor has said "Yes," but he must
> still talk to Bethmann Hollweg. What will
> be the attitude of his Majesty [the Austrian
> Emperor]?
> MYSELF: If Germany agrees his Majesty
> will be for war against Serbia.

. . . . .

> COUNT BERCHTOLD: Tisza is against the
> war. He fears a Rumanian invasion of
> Transylvania. What happens in Galicia
> when we mobilize against Serbia?
> MYSELF: In Galicia we shall not mobilize
> for the present. But if there is a threat from
> Russia we shall have to mobilize the three
> Galician Army Corps.
> COUNT FORGACH: I do not doubt that
> Germany will go with us; it is her duty as
> an ally, and, moreover, her own existence is
> at stake.
> MYSELF: When can I get the German
> reply?
> COUNT BERCHTOLD: To-morrow. But
> the Germans will ask us what is to happen
> after the war.

Myself: Tell them, then, that we do not know ourselves.

But Germany asked no questions. Hoyos could report that she left Austria a free hand and would unreservedly stand by her. Tisza alone had doubts and asked questions. After the Cabinet Council of July 7, in which all the others demanded war, he addressed a Memorandum to the Emperor registering his dissent. " In all probability such an attack against Serbia would provoke the intervention of Russia and therefore the world war, in which case, in spite of Berlin optimism, I would consider Rumania's neutrality at least doubtful." Altogether he considered the diplomatic position in Europe most unfavourable to Austria-Hungary, and urged that a moderate, not a threatening, Note should be sent to Serbia, and the possibility left to her to accept a diplomatic defeat. " In spite of my devotion to your Majesty's service, or rather because of it, I am unable to share in the responsibility for an exclusively and aggressively warlike *dénouement*."

Meantime the war party proceeded with its plans. On July 8 Berchtold informed Conrad that a short-term ultimatum would be presented to Serbia.

Count Berchtold: What happens if Serbia lets it come to a mobilization and then gives in on every point?

MYSELF: Then we march into Serbia.

COUNT BERCHTOLD: Yes — but if Serbia does nothing at all?

MYSELF: Then we shall remain there till our expenses are paid.

COUNT BERCHTOLD: We shall put our ultimatum only after the harvest and the Serajevo inquiry are concluded.

MYSELF: Better to-day than to-morrow; so long as the situation remains what it is. If our opponents get wind, they will prepare.

COUNT BERCHTOLD: Care will be taken that the secret is preserved. . . .

MYSELF: When is the ultimatum to be sent?

COUNT BERCHTOLD: In a fortnight. On July 22. It would be good if you and the Minister for War went on leave, so as to give the impression that nothing is happening.

Conrad cordially endorsed this view — " Everything has to be avoided which might alarm our opponents and make them take counter-measures; on the contrary, a peaceful complexion must be put on everything." Therefore on July 14 he and the Minister for War went on leave, which was to be broken off in eight days, *i.e.* simultaneously with the presenting of the ultimatum.

Events and conversations are recorded in Conrad's book in a steady, indiscriminate flow, true to life; so that, just as in life, one finds it difficult to fix the moment when decisions ripened until suddenly they are treated as irrevocable. A week earlier the question of Germany's co-operation seemed in doubt; next the German Emperor was made to commit himself; and in the end his promise came to be considered binding on Austria. Berchtold, who went to see the Emperor at Ischl on July 9, reported to have found him " very determined and calm. His Majesty seemed for action against Serbia and merely feared possible troubles in Hungary [obviously from the non-Magyar nationalities]. Nor could one now draw back any more, be it merely because of Germany. Tisza pleads for caution and is against the war; but Baron Burian has gone to Budapest to talk to him."

How Tisza was finally persuaded to agree remains a mystery even now. From none of the disclosures and publications made hitherto, not even from Conrad's, emerges a fully satisfactory answer. At the Cabinet Council of July 19 Tisza agreed to war, merely demanding a solemn and unanimous resolution that no annexations would be made in Serbia — he feared for Magyar dominion should any further Slav territories be included in the Habsburg Monarchy.

The ultimatum to Serbia was postponed by a day because Berchtold preferred to wait until President Poincaré had left Petrograd. It was presented on July 23 at 6 P.M., and even before the prescribed 48 hours had elapsed, on July 25 at 8 A.M., on (uncertain) news of a Serb mobilization, Conrad was already pressing for a mobilization order; " where strategic considerations arise, it is for me to make the suggestions and the rest does not concern me." The same night eight Army Corps — *i.e.* half the Austro-Hungarian Army — were mobilized. The ball was set rolling; it was the mobilization demanded by the Chiefs of Staff, each of them afraid lest his opponent might steal a march on him, which finally overrode the hesitations of various diplomatists and frustrated the urgent endeavours of Sir Edward Grey to save the peace of Europe; the military were making their suggestions, and " the rest did not concern them." It is about the mobilization of the Central Powers that the present volume of Conrad supplies most valuable information, and, on the diplomatic side, this is, in fact, the most remarkable contribution which it makes to our knowledge about the origins of the war.

When Austria-Hungary mobilized half her Army, Russia on her part began to prepare for mobilization, declaring, however, that she would not mobilize unless the Austrian troops crossed the Serbian frontier. When on July 28 Austria-Hungary declared war on Serbia, Russia mobilized the military districts of Kiev, Odessa, Moscow, and Kazan.

On July 30 the German Ambassador informed Berchtold of the British offer of mediation *à quatre*, adding the urgent request of the German Cabinet that Austria-Hungary " should accept England's mediation under these honourable conditions." With this Note, Berchtold, Conrad, and the Minister for War went to the Emperor. The question was discussed what should now be demanded of Serbia.

> She would have to accept our ulti-matum word for word and repay all the expenses arising from the mobilization.
>
> I added that territorial cessions would have to be demanded, such as would at least secure our military position: Belgrade and Sabac with the adjoining territory for the raising of extensive fortifications, for which, too, Serbia would have to pay.
>
> The EMPEROR: They will never agree to that.
>
> COUNT BERCHTOLD: Further, Count Tisza has demanded that we should not ask for any cessions of territory.
>
> I rejoined that we could not stop opera-tions against Serbia when all was in progress; it would be impossible as the Army would not stand it. We would have to tell Ger-many — If Russia mobilizes, we too, would have to mobilize.

The upshot of the talk with the Emperor is summarized as follows:

> War against Serbia is to be continued.
> The British offer is to receive a very polite answer but without its substance being accepted.
> General mobilization is to be ordered on August 1 with August 4 as the first day of mobilization; but this was to be talked over further the next day (July 31).

Then for a moment it seemed as if the Emperor William thought of drawing back, and as if there had been a change in the attitude of Berlin owing to the dropping out of Italy. Conrad's representative in the information bureau of the German General Staff wired to him on July 30 after a talk with Moltke:

> Russian mobilization no reason yet for mobilizing; only on outbreak of war between Austria-Hungary and Russia. In contradistinction to the by now customary Russian mobilizations and demobilizations, German mobilization would unavoidably lead to war. Do not declare war on Russia but await Russian attack.

To this Conrad replied: " We shall not declare war on Russia nor start the war."

But a telegram received the same day at 7 P.M.

238

from the Austrian Ambassador in Berlin "dispelled our fears concerning Germany's attitude. We were informed that Germany had declared on Sunday at Petrograd that Russian mobilization would be followed by a German mobilization."

On the morning of July 31 I was informed by the Foreign Office that Germany would address an ultimatum to Russia concerning her military preparations. My above telegram to General von Moltke, dispatched on July 30, crossed another telegram from Moltke received by us on July 31 at 7.45 A.M.; it ran as follows: "Face Russian mobilization: Austria - Hungary must be preserved, mobilize immediately against Russia. Germany will mobilize. By compensations compel Italy to do her duty as ally."

Further the following telegram was received from our Military Attaché at Berlin: "Moltke says that he considers the position critical if Austria-Hungary does not immediately mobilize against Russia. Russia's declaration concerning ordered mobilization renders necessary Austro-Hungarian counter-measures, which is to be mentioned in published explanation. This would constitute treaty case for Germany. With Italy reach honest agreement by giving compensations so that Italy remains actively on the side of Triple Alliance, by no means leave a single

239

man on Italian frontier. Refuse renewed English *démarche* for maintenance of peace. For Austria-Hungary enduring of European war last measure of self-preservation. Germany absolutely stands by her."

I went with these wires to the Minister for War and with him to Count Berchtold, where we met Count Tisza, Count Stuergkh, and Baron Burian. After I had read out the wires, Count Berchtold exclaimed: "*Dan ist gelungen!* (This is excellent!) Who rules: Moltke or Bethmann? "

Berchtold then read out the following telegram from the German Emperor to the Emperor Francis Joseph, received at Schoenbrunn on July 30 at 8 P.M.: "I did not think it possible to refuse personal request from Russian Emperor to make an attempt at mediation with a view to avoiding world conflagration and maintaining world peace, and I have yesterday and to-day instructed my Ambassador to submit proposals to your Government. Among other things they suggest that Austria after occupation of Belgrade and other places should make known her conditions. I should be most grateful if you could let me have your decision as soon as possible. In most faithful friendship, WILLIAM."

.   .   .   .   .

Count Berchtold having read the telegram turned towards me saying: " I have

A CARTOON BY MAX BEERBOHM
1926

asked you to come here, because I had the impression that Germany was drawing back; but now I have received from the most authoritative military quarter the most reassuring declaration."

Thereupon it was decided to ask his Majesty to order a general mobilization.

This was issued the same day at 12.23 P.M. But meanwhile Conrad's telegram saying that Austria-Hungary would not declare war on Russia nor start the war had reached Moltke and elicited from him the following reply, received in Vienna on July 31 at 7.15 P.M.: " Will Austria desert Germany? "

Conrad had, of course, no difficulty in answering this. Events had outpaced the wires.

But for the time being Austria refrained from declaring war on France and England, not from any special sympathy, but from fear lest her own fleet should be caught unprepared. An interesting scheme was then discussed of sending it, together with the *Goeben* and *Breslau*, into the Black Sea, where, by securing the Roumanian and Bulgarian coasts and by attacking that of Russia, it was expected to help in getting these two Balkan States into the war on the side of the Central Powers. This scheme had, however, to be dropped because the Admiral commanding the Austro-Hungarian Fleet declared it impracticable and the Fleet insufficiently prepared for it. Meantime Berchtold twice assured France (on August 9 and 10) that no Austro-Hungarian troops had been sent to the Western front, though on the same days Moltke was thanking Conrad for the heavy howitzers sent to Belgium.

Moltke had recommended an " honest arrangement " with Italy which would have secured her help at the price of the Trentino. At one time, but only for a moment, Conrad himself seemed to have dallied with the idea, adding that " after a successful war one perfidy could be repaid by another and the Trentino could be retaken from the blackmailers " — with which the honest Moltke seems to have agreed, as he on his own initiative advised the Austrian representative at German G.H.Q. to pay the price of the Trentino. " Once the war with Russia is finished you can always challenge Italy, and Germany will stand by you."

On the outbreak of war, on August 5, Moltke addressed a cordial letter to Conrad which started with the admission that " our proceedings in Belgium are certainly brutal, but it is a question of life and death, and who gets into our way has to bear the consequences," and finished with a hearty Teuton " Mit Gott, mein Herr Kamerad! " The third postscript to this letter ran as follows:

Gather all your strength against Russia. Even the Italians cannot be such mean dogs as to stab you in the back. Unleash the Bulgars against Serbia and let that rabble kill off each other. Now there is but one goal for you: Russia! Drive these knout-bearers into the Pripet marshes and drown them. — Yours ever, MOLTKE.

In a letter of August 13 Conrad reciprocated these fantasies:

Will Germany let the six English Divisions land on the Continent without a naval battle? Splendid it would be to catch the transports and sink them.

They were indeed to drown *currum et aurigam*; they merely failed to foresee which.

BARON MUSULIN [1]

("*The Times Literary Supplement,*" *August* 20, 1925)

MORE expressive of ruin even than the Imperial Vienna Hofburg, uninhabited and stripped of pomp and glory, is the House at the Ballplatz, the Austrian Foreign Office, where the business of the present Austria continues to be transacted. Once it was inhabited by men who wielded power; Kaunitz had worked there, and Metternich. From this house the ultimatum of July 23, 1914, was issued which set the world ablaze; now there come from it only appeals for help on behalf of a ruined city. The title of Baron Musulin's book and its motto—" *Fuimus Troes* . . ." — speak the same language.

Baron Musulin is known to have prepared the draft of the ultimatum to Serbia; and his memoirs are an apologia which is convincing where it is not conscious, but breaks down when it reaches that one fortnight in his life in which he came to deal with matters of supreme importance. He appears in his autobiography as a simple, honest man who

---

[1] Freiherr von Musulin, " Das Haus am Ballplatz."

did not think very deeply or aim very high, but
took the chances and pleasures of life, and with
judgment and understanding fulfilled the duties
of the posts he held. Only in his account of July
1914 he seems to shrink below normal stature,
and conveys the impression of a very peculiar,
indeed surprising, insufficiency of mind and
memory. His defence is this: that in drafting
the ultimatum he acted merely as an amanuensis,
and that neither he nor anyone else knew what
they were doing. " It was the tragedy of my
career," writes Baron Musulin, " to have risen
sufficiently high to see how things happened, but
not sufficiently high to have a share in the decisions. Things happened under my eyes but not
through me."

A Croat by birth, of an army family, he entered
the Austro-Hungarian diplomatic service in 1892,
remaining abroad till 1903, when he was transferred to the Eastern Department in the Vienna
Foreign Office.

This appointment I owed to having
served at the posts which counted most in
the active policy of the Foreign Office —
St. Petersburg, Bucharest, and Belgrade.
Moreover, my various chiefs abroad attri-
buted to me a certain ability for office work
and stylistic skill in writing both German and
French. For my own part I was conscious

of my limitations. What I lacked was the
gift of imagination. . . .

From 1910 till 1916 he was chief of the comparatively unimportant Department for Church
Affairs. But in the summer of 1913, after many
years of absence, he revisited his native country,
and on his return to the Foreign Office wrote a
report on the Yugoslav problem and on Serb propaganda. This presumably must have had something to do with his being asked some time in
July 1914 — Baron Musulin does not remember
the day — to draft a Note " wherein, on the basis
of Serbia's moral responsibility for the events of
June 28 [the murder of the Archduke], certain
demands were to be addressed to her for the sup-
pression in future of Great-Serb propaganda."
Baron Musulin, however, thinks that he was
chosen because of his reputation for " abilities for
office work and stylistic skill." In his account he
represents the Austrian statesmen responsible for
the ultimatum as anxiously asking themselves
with regard to every article whether Serbia could
accept it, and states that on none was the discussion
closed until this question had been answered in
the affirmative. According to him, it was generally thought in the Austrian Foreign Office that
Serbia would accept the ultimatum, and he claims
that surprise was felt at the sharp criticism with

which it met abroad. " It is altogether difficult to foresee the effect which any one political action will produce abroad " — certainly if one is deficient in the " gift of imagination."

Here, then, is another of those average, personally honest, well-meaning men whom a dark fate had chosen for pawns in the game that was to result in the greatest disaster of European history. He did not think independently about the matters with which he was called upon to deal; and his very manner of acting seems to have been subordinate in character, automatic, determined by preconceived ideas and the influence of his surroundings. Overwhelmed by the consequences, of which the magnitude is out of all proportion to his own person and influence, he rightly pleads how small and insignificant his own part has been, but forgets how many of those with whom he then acted could say the same, how many of them could describe themselves as mere amanuenses of a force which seemed external to them. And yet without their collective help even that malignant, narrow, and purblind military politician, Field-Marshal Conrad von Hötzendorf, could not have had his war. Baron Musulin ignores Conrad's admissions about the policy of the ultimatum and Tisza's protests against it, but clutches at anything which may serve to suggest that war was not its necessary consequence. Thus he gives prominence to the idea propounded to him by Count Tisza some time in July 1914, that, provided the territorial integrity and sovereignty of Serbia were respected, Russia would refrain from real war against Austria-Hungary and " limit herself to a kind of warlike demonstration (*Scheinkrieg*), which would then very soon be concluded by a compromise honourable to both sides." Obviously Count Tisza, having agreed to the ultimatum against his own better judgment, comforted himself with this idea, trying to hide the future from his own seeing eyes. Baron Musulin has now woven Tisza's argument into the curtain of oblivion which to his own mind is to cover the past; he, who actually drafted that historic ultimatum, if pressed for more information, might perhaps say with as much honesty as does Pilate, in his old age, in Anatole France's " Procurateur de Judée ": " Jésus de Nazareth? Je ne me rappelle pas."

COUNT STEPHEN TISZA [1]

(" *The Times Literary Supplement*," *April* 19, 1928)

COUNT STEPHEN TISZA, Hungarian Prime Minister at the outbreak of the war, was the strongest man in the Habsburg Monarchy and one of the very few among its statesmen with whom even Germany had to count. He was at first opposed to the measures which brought on the war; what was it, that about the middle of July 1914, made him give way to Berchtold, Conrad, and other irresponsible warmongers? To this question even his letters fail to supply an answer; but they confirm — what was obvious to those acquainted with Tisza's views and mentality — that he did not object to the war policy as such, but merely to the moment chosen for action. He wrote on August 27, 1914:

> Twenty bitter years I was oppressed by the idea that this Monarchy, and with it the Magyar nation, were doomed to perdition, for the Lord means to destroy those whom he

[1] " Graf Stefan Tisza: Briefe," edited by Oskar von Wertheimer, vol. i.

deprives of reason. During the last few years
things began to take a turn for the better.
Again and again joyous events awakened a
hope of new life: a hope that history will
not after all coldly dismiss us. Now, in these
momentous days, will be reached the decision.

Thus to Tisza the old peace policy of Austria-
Hungary, and not the new turn which it had
received since 1908, appeared as demented.

Tisza, for one, clearly realized to what an
extent the fate of the Magyar State was bound
up with the survival of the Habsburg Monarchy.
While the " Dualist " structure of the Monarchy
and the Hungarian constitution effectively precluded any far-reaching Habsburg intervention in
Hungary's internal affairs, it enabled Magyar
statesmen, leaders of a nation of nine millions, to
rule the other nationalities of Hungary with a rod
of iron, and at the same time to direct the foreign
policy of a Great Power. One would search in
vain in these letters for any trace of that " bond-
age " which, since the war, the Magyars allege they
had lived in before 1918, so as to establish their
alibi with regard to a policy crowned with disaster.
It was the Magyars who directed Austria-
Hungary's foreign policy; and, according to
Tisza, they alone were fit to do so. Thus, on
August 11, 1914, he wrote to Burian, at that time
his representative at Vienna (Hungarian Minister

a latere): " If the Monarchy is to preserve its capacity for action and its political level, the deciding influence in foreign affairs has to remain with the Magyar nation." But not in private letters alone did he state this view, which could hardly have been palatable to the Austrians; in a circular issued on December 31, 1914, to the heads of the Hungarian counties, Tisza inserted the following brief and significant statement: " The power of the [Magyar] nation and its decisive influence on the fate of the Monarchy must grow in proportion to its sacrifices and exertions." And at the end of April 1915, replying to an alleged message from Sonnino, he declared:

> The lasting friendship between Italy and Hungary is the natural outcome of common interests and feelings, and the preponderance of the Hungarian element in the direction of Austria-Hungary's policy ensures that her diplomatic and military activities will never be directed against Italy.

Magyar preponderance was the inevitable result of political conditions within the two Habsburg States. There were two Prime Ministers in the hyphenated Austro-Hungarian Monarchy and only one Foreign Minister, who was not a member of either Cabinet and in theory had to carry out the policy of both; but while Austria's internal in-

coherence and the decay of her Parliamentary
institutions had reduced her Prime Minister to
the level of an official (which he usually was by
antecedents), the Magyars, by effectively de-
priving the other nationalities of Hungary of their
due representation in the Budapest Parliament,
had succeeded in preserving the appearances of a
strongly-welded national State and in establishing
a firm Parliamentary Government. The Foreign
Minister could ignore the Austrian Prime Minister, but when on one occasion Burian, Tisza's representative, was refused information even though
merely about a matter of secondary importance
(Berchtold feeling bound by a promise of absolute
secrecy), Tisza wrote to Berchtold on September 4, 1914:

> I agree with you that the present case is
> of small practical importance. This does
> not, however, absolve me of the duty to
> emphasize that even the severest discretion
> and secrecy cannot extend to the Hungarian
> Prime Minister. I, too, am responsible for
> the foreign policy; it is my task, as repre-
> senting the Hungarian State, to exercise its
> legal influence, and I can serve only with a
> Foreign Minister whom I can fully trust to
> withhold nothing whatsoever from me.

By the beginning of 1915, in view of the
negotiations with Italy, Tisza decided that a

change was necessary at the Foreign Office. He therefore went to Vienna, and, on January 10, informed Berchtold of what he was going to say to the Emperor: that a stronger, more determined man had to be put in his place. Thereupon Berchtold, " in his usual manner of a good child . . . replied, laughing: ' I am awfully grateful to you if you tell him that. I say it all the time, but he does not believe me. If you say so, he will.' " The " good child " now gaily left the Foreign Office, which was offered by the Emperor to Tisza. But Tisza thought: " Also from my present position I can influence foreign policy," and advised the Emperor to appoint Burian. " I added, that it would perhaps reassure his Majesty . . . that he [Burian] agreed with me in all important matters, and was a close friend of mine, so that we were sure of intimate, harmonious co-operation." And he advised Burian to have a special telephone connexion with himself installed in his new office.

The war had broken out over the problem of the Habsburg dominions; both Italy and Rumania had territorial claims against them, but were bound by traditional friendships and economic ties to Germany. In these circumstances it was natural that the German Foreign Office should take the lead in the vital diplomatic negotiations with these two Powers; but, if they were to be bought

off, Austria-Hungary would have to foot the bill.
Germany had no objection to sacrificing scraps
of Austrian territory — the Trentino to Italy, and
part of the Bukovina to Rumania; moreover, she
desired concessions to be made by Hungary to
the Transylvanian Rumanians. Austria was a
corpse; there was no common life or organic
unity in her body, and the Habsburgs were always
ready to barter territories — now they had their
eyes fixed on Russian Poland. But Hungary was
a historic and geographical unit, and to the
Magyars every square foot of territory belonging
to the Lands of the Crown of St. Stephen was
sacrosanct; and though they had no feeling about
Austrian territory, they resisted cessions to Italy
and Rumania; for if once that game was started,
what certainty was there that it could be stopped
at the frontiers of Hungary? And as for inter-
ference in internal Hungarian affairs, Tisza, while
assuring the Germans that he himself meant to
meet the wishes of the Rumanians of Transylvania,
refused to have either the extent or the time of his
concessions prescribed by Berlin.

> I must ask you insistently [he wrote to
> Berchtold on September 4, 1914, in reply
> to German suggestions in that matter] not to
> take Tschirschky [the German Ambassador
> at Vienna] tragically. It is his custom to
> " climb about on superlatives." As far as I

know, nothing as yet has come direct from Berlin, but even were it so, we could face matters calmly. Germany needs us as much as we need her. Threats between us are ridiculous. There is no occasion for frights. No one can value the German alliance higher than I do. We must render it most valuable to them by loyalty and the greatest possible exertions; such German attempts at preponderance must, however, be met in a friendly, calm, determined manner.

In the dealings with Italy, the Central Powers had the active support of the Pope, who, in conjunction with Prince Bülow and Erzberger, practically prescribed what cessions Austria-Hungary should make — not an easy position for the unfortunate Macchio, the Austro-Hungarian Ambassador to the Quirinal. On May 9 Erzberger wired from Rome to Berlin:

> Developments have convinced me of necessity definitely to exclude Macchio. Please insist that Vienna instructs him to-day to get ill. He must not leave his house any more nor receive visits, or else he intrigues. . . . There can be no mercy or pity for Macchio, or regard for Vienna.

But next day, under pressure from the Germans, the Vatican, and Giolitti, Macchio made the concessions they demanded. These Tisza considered

excessive; and, although they could not be withdrawn any more, he telephoned to Burian:

> . . . I request you to send immediately
> instructions to Macchio forbidding him to
> make further concessions beyond those
> authorized by us, and ordering him to try
> with all his strength to reach favourable re-
> sults on open points, whilst maintaining
> positive promises he has made in our name.

And on May 15 Erzberger wired through the
German Embassy to Father Count Andlau in
Vienna:

> Best thanks for your successful endea-
> vours. His Holiness thanks you most
> warmly. He has declared . . . that he must
> consider any withdrawal of these concessions
> by Austria as personally slighting him, as his
> Holiness has most particularly pleaded in
> favour of this Austrian offer.

After the efforts had failed and Italy had
entered the war, the Germans accused Austria-
Hungary of having lost the game by refusing
cessions of territory when the Germans thought a
bargain could have been struck; while Vienna
and Budapest accused the Germans of having
destroyed the value of any offer they could make
by freely running ahead of it. It seems highly
probable that this combination of Germany's

eagerness to make concessions at the expense of her ally, and of Magyar stubbornness in refusing them, had the worst possible effect; but the game was lost beforehand. Small concessions could not satisfy Italy, which looked to great gains, while large ones could not satisfy her either, as she could not have trusted a victorious Austria-Hungary to abide by such a settlement. Italy's entry into the war was merely a question of time, and it was likely to be encouraged by a Russian victory, and as likely to be hastened by a Russian defeat, which would have endangered her chances. When once a problem reaches a stage at which contrary developments are apt to produce equally unfavourable results, it is doubtful whether any man can save the situation.

COUNT JULIUS ANDRASSY, Junior [1]

THE Magyars had no frontier and no quarrel with the Western Powers; their dominion within the historic borders of Hungary was challenged by Russia, Rumania, and Serbia. Dependent as they were on Germany for protection against their neighbours, they could but deplore her pursuing policies which brought her into conflict with France and England. They themselves at all times have been prone to engage in innocuous flirtations with the West-European Powers. But "Hungary's policy is determined by laws as precise and permanent as the laws of nature," declared Count Andrassy at Munich on May 16, 1916. "The Germans support us, and we are to them a protecting wall." And again in the Hungarian Parliament, on June 20, 1918: "The Germans are the only great nation in whose interest it is that there should be a strong Hungary." [2] Indeed, there is no other basis for an

[1] Count Julius Andrassy, "Diplomatie und Weltkrieg" (1920). An English translation of the book appeared in 1921.
[2] Naturally this thesis is not reproduced in the book pub-

258

active Magyar policy, and the Imperialisms of the two races stand and fall together.

Count Andrassy, as the son of one of the greatest statesmen of the preceding generation, was, from his early youth, conversant with European affairs; later on, he was Minister or " *ministeriable*." After German and Magyar Imperialisms had jointly collapsed in October 1918, he was able to write a frank and dispassionate review of the more remote origins of the war. In his book he observes the Western Powers without hatred or envy. On points of detail he does justice even to Russia, nay, even to Serbia; he admits, for instance, that no ground whatsoever had been shown by the judicial inquiry for suspecting the Serbian Government of complicity in the Serajevo murder. But a convenient blindness affects the Magyar where the wider aspects of Russian policy, and still more, where Yugo-Slav national aspirations are concerned.

About the immediate causes of the war, all that Andrassy has to say is that Serbia coveted territory which belonged to Austria-Hungary. So did Piedmont in 1848; but would anyone consider this a sufficient analysis of that problem? Although Andrassy admits that Austria-Hungary had repeatedly thwarted Serbia's national am-

lished at the time of Germany's weakness; nor was it otherwise much heard about till after Germany's recovery.

COUNT JULIUS ANDRASSY, JUNIOR

bitions, he is careful not to ask himself by what
right the 9 million Magyars were barring the way
to the national reunion of 13 million Yugo-Slavs,
and of the Rumanians, Czecho-Slovaks, and Little
Russians as well. And he thus justifies his father's
action in occupying Bosnia-Herzegovina in 1878,
after the Yugo-Slav national movement had under-
mined Turkey's dominion over these provinces:

> The acquisition of Bosnia-Herzegovina
> would not have satisfied the Serbs, it would
> have merely encouraged them . . . to stretch
> out their hands for Dalmatia and Croatia.
> . . . The nearer Serbia approached the sea,
> the keener would she have been to reach it.
> It would have been harder to renounce Zara,
> Ragusa, and Cattaro for a Serbia bordering
> on Dalmatia than while the River Drina [the
> Eastern border of Bosnia] remained her
> frontier. A better chance of attaining Yugo-
> Slav unity would have increased the desire
> for it at Belgrade.

Not even the unity of a common subjection were
the Magyars prepared to concede to the Yugo-
Slavs. " It was almost an axiom with us," says
Andrassy, " that there were already enough non-
Magyars in Hungary " (hence the lack of appetite
for further annexations). Moreover, " the Serbs
accustomed to independence would never have
fitted themselves into their new position. In vain

260

should we have established Yugo-Slav unity; they would have used it only to break away and establish their independence." [1]

During the Bosnian Crisis of 1908–9, Andrassy, then Hungarian Minister of the Interior, criticized Count Aehrenthal's policy, and wished for stronger action against Serbia, apparently agreeing therein with Conrad von Hötzendorf:

> I wanted to settle accounts with Serbia and impose on her a convention stipulating for a disarmament of her forces. . . . Russia was not as yet prepared for intervention. . . . I considered that Serbia would have had to give in. . . . Had she resisted, she would have stood alone. . . . This view I recorded in a minority opinion on the minutes of the Cabinet.

[1] The same view was put forward by Count Tisza, Hungarian Prime Minister, in a report to the Emperor on December 5, 1915. To him an annexation of all Serbia seemed destructive of the Magyar national State: " I emphatically deny that the incorporation of all Serbia would put an end to the Russian and Serb intrigues against the Monarchy, and that by the sacrifice of the Hungarian national State the Serbs at least could permanently be attached to the Monarchy. . . . The union of all Serbs under one sceptre, the strengthening of the Serb element as against the other nationalities, the creation of a considerable majority of Greek-Orthodox Serbs as against the [Roman-Catholic] Croats, all this would merely encourage the Great-Serbian agitation. Any concession made to their nationalism would be used as a weapon in the struggle for their ultimate aim: to break away from the [Habsburg] Monarchy."

The need of crushing Serbia was an axiom with Andrassy. On July 30, 1914, Austria-Hungary was prepared, under certain conditions, to accept mediation, but " we did not abandon the idea of defeating the Serbian army." " We . . . did not want the World War . . . but we wanted to defeat Serbia." Austria-Hungary had " to settle by arms her accounts with Serbia." In October 1915 Andrassy advised Herr von Bethmann Hollweg to make a public offer of peace, " *i.e.* once Serbia is crushed." [1] He thought it possible to settle the differences between the Great Powers — and then Hungary would be free to deal with Serbia. There were 9 million Magyars and more than 70 million Germans; and Ludendorff was merely a much larger Andrassy, with more varied interests and half the world for his Serbia.

During the war, Andrassy was debarred from office by the bitter hostility which divided him from Tisza. After that iron fighter had withdrawn in despair, the pleasant and feeble Andrassy became, on October 25, 1918, Austro-Hungarian Minister for Foreign Affairs, and began devising half-measures. Lack of deeper insight, a sense of

[1] Again there is little difference between the " liberal-minded " Andrassy and the " reactionary " Tisza. According to Bishop Fraknoi, Tisza, in the first days of December 1915, went to Berlin and tried to convince the Emperor William of the need for a speedy, " moderate " peace.

duty, and his lifelong ambition to fill the post once held by his father, may have moved him to accept office, though there was nothing left for him to do; and this was his first and most fundamental blunder. Having accepted office, he had to profess a belief in possibilities which did not exist, and on October 27 offered a separate peace to the Allies, when such an offer could no longer be of any interest to them; and in his Note he acknowledged the existence of Czecho-Slovakia and Yugo-Slavia as nations at war with the Central Powers, a serious lapse in logic and tactics. Not that it mattered much what he did, or did not, acknowledge; yet this Note sounded the death-knell of Austria-Hungary, and in Vienna itself finally destroyed the position of the Habsburgs, as the Austrian Germans bitterly resented that gratuitous abandonment of Germany. And now in his book, Count Andrassy commits his third mistake: he makes pathetic attempts to justify his policy.

On October 11, 1918, he states, he was told by the Emperor " that it would be possible for him confidentially to negotiate peace in Switzerland with Allied diplomatists." Having gone there he found that " this information was out of date, and that the position had changed." " The Allied diplomatists would have been prepared to speak to me only had I been officially authorized to negotiate and conclude an agreement." On October 18, Andrassy seems still to have been at Berne with " several Austro-Polish and Magyar politicians," and it is presumably from them that he derived this information, on which he apparently based his " policy " after assuming office. "Count Czernin has lied," said Clemenceau in reply to another Austro-Hungarian Foreign Minister, when he made similar allegations. This would be much too harsh a word to use for Count Andrassy — he is merely talking through his hat.

GENERAL ARZ [1]

GENERAL ARZ succeeded Conrad von Hötzendorf
as the last Chief of the Austro-Hungarian General
Staff on March 1, 1917, and left the post only
after both the Empire and the army had vanished.
The first part of his memoirs recounts his ex-
periences as commander on the Russian and
Rumanian fronts; the second covers the period
of spurious triumphs, when Austria-Hungary,
broken and exhausted, towered over hostile neighbours whom she had not beaten down, and
anxiously wondered how long this paradoxical
position could endure; the last part contains the
tale of the final disaster, when the Germans no
longer could help or bully, and mere echoes from
the Western front sufficed to destroy hollow shams
in East-Central Europe.

In character General Arz differed widely from
his predecessor and his German colleagues. He
had neither the solid simplicity of Hindenburg,
nor the snarling, aggressive energy of Ludendorff,
nor the verbose ingenuity and conceit of Conrad

[1] General Arz, "Zur Geschichte des Grossen Krieges,
1914–1918."

265

von Hötzendorf; he is never impressive and always polite. About the enemy he says next to nothing, but whenever he mentions anyone on his own side, a flattering *epitheton ornans* invariably accompanies the name. In a way it is a relief to find a man who does not break out in accusations against those whom " misery hath joined in equal ruin," nor argues that had his advice and warnings been heeded, victory would have been achieved. But could any one with marked personality be so invariably appreciative, even-tempered, and discreet? Arz was probably the right man for the post when he attained it; possessed of a fair amount of ability and experience, he did not think himself a genius, nor did he yearn for magnificent adventure; he offended nobody, and did not interfere with Germany's war-work or Vienna's peace intrigues; in short, he proved adaptable and accommodating.

Whatever was left of the Austro-Hungarian army after the Galician and Serbian defeats of 1914 and the Luck catastrophe of June 1916, had been subordinated to the German Supreme Command — " I felt no difficulty," writes Arz, " in placing myself under the authority of a leader so great and glorious as Hindenburg, who had an assistant of the genius of Ludendorff, especially as I could always frankly express to them my opinion." By the end of February 1917, Austria-

Hungary had lost 576,898 officers and men killed, and 1,361,423 prisoners or missing; of the remaining 3½ millions only 780,000 were combatants. Even so the numbers left to do the most indispensable work in factories, mines, and agriculture were insufficient, and the shortage of necessaries was destroying both "the home front" and the army. But by 1917 the only serious task which still faced Austria was a counter-offensive against Italy. This the Austrian army command wished to carry out entirely on its own. "Surely you will understand," wrote the Emperor Charles to the Emperor William on August 26, 1917, " my attaching special importance to the offensive against Italy being carried out exclusively by my own troops. My entire army calls the war against Italy ' our war.' " But the Germans had their doubts, and the Caporetto offensive was duly carried out with German " collaboration."

However much General Arz concedes in this part of his book about the precarious position of the Habsburg Monarchy and the material shortcomings of its armies, he does not admit the full truth, perhaps not even to himself; only when the general catastrophe sets in, in the summer of 1918, his narrative becomes unrestrained and perfectly sincere, and therefore most interesting. A fairly full account of the material collapse of the Habsburg Monarchy is given by the man who

was at that time in charge of its material organization. The trite phraseology and would-be epic
elaboration of the earlier chapters recedes, and
there remains the pain and worry of one who
honestly, with all his strength and heart-felt devotion, served the cause in which he had been
taught to believe.

General Arz did not concern himself with
politics more than was necessary; unlike Field-
Marshal Conrad, he did not lecture Foreign
Secretaries on problems of international policy,
nor talk of *coups d'état* within the Dual Monarchy.
He too has the Austrian " *malformation militaire*,"
but in its most innocuous variation — just on
proper occasions he comes out with appropriate
cant learnt in forty years of army service. At the
front the Emperor Charles meets " the best part
of the nation . . . united in the common high
purpose to defend the unity of the Empire " (but
in the very next sentence Arz admits that " as
time went on, the voices which loudly proclaimed
the great idea of maintaining the unity of centuries
had become very few, and it was doubtful whether
these voices reached those who had to sacrifice
their blood and treasure for the idea "). On
August 17, 1917, ". . . the armed forces . . .
celebrate the birthday of their All-Highest War
Lord. The nations of Austria-Hungary pray for
the well-being of the beloved Emperor and

King "; and a year later on the same day, the Austro-Hungarian Field-Marshals, on behalf of the armies, pray the Emperor Charles to accept the *bâton* of a Field-Marshal. But eleven weeks later, on St. Charles' Day, the Austro-Hungarian armies are no more; they have gone to their own national homes, casting out the memory of Austria-Hungary and obliterating the boundaries and signs of her past existence. Only a handful of young cadets and old officers — General Arz among them — to whom the Habsburg Monarchy had been their home and their all, on November 4, 1918, in the Schönbrunn Palace Chapel for the last time sang the Imperial Hymn.

T. E. LAWRENCE

T. E. LAWRENCE

a photograph by Flight-Lieutenant R. G. Sims, R.A.F., at Hornsea, Yorkshire,
February 1935; probably the last portrait taken of him

LAWRENCE: AS I KNEW HIM

[I wrote this essay on the day of Lawrence's death, at the request of the " Manchester Guardian," in which it appeared on May 20, 1935. I added to it when it was reprinted in the collection of essays, " T. E. Lawrence by His Friends " (edited by A. W. Lawrence and published by Jonathan Cape). My excuse for reprinting it a second time is that it seems to form a necessary introduction to the two reviews (which follow) of " The Seven Pillars of Wisdom " and " The Letters of T. E. Lawrence." These, as well as his letters to his two biographers, Mr. Robert Graves and Captain Liddell Hart, contain a mass of new material, and with its help I at first intended further to expand my essay. I soon found, however, that this would destroy its balance and completely change its character; and I have finished by removing even some of the additions which I had made when it was first reprinted. If time and circumstances permit, I would much rather attempt a new and more extensive study of T. E. Lawrence, based on all his printed works, his letters, and on as yet unprinted material.]

I HAD a slight acquaintance with Lawrence in our undergraduate days but knew nothing about him. A day or two after war had been declared he took me to a disused rifle range in North Oxford to practise shooting.[1] I do not remember how I fell in with him that day, nor where he got the rifle, and it strikes me only now that this cannot have been his first visit to the range. With what plans or dreams had he been practising there?

After that for several years I heard nothing of him, for only when I met him in the lounge of the Hotel Majestic at the Paris Conference in a colonel's uniform did I realize that he was " Lawrence of Arabia."

It was in 1920, when I was at Balliol and he at All Souls, that I came to know him. He was accessible and communicative, and there must be hundreds of people who have known him as well as I, or better. He was retiring and yet craved to be seen, he was sincerely shy and naïvely exhibitionist. He had to rise above others, and then humble himself, and in his self-inflicted humiliation demonstrate his superiority. It was a mysterious game which he had started long before he became a private. It amused or puzzled some, annoyed or put off others. He himself enjoyed it in a quaint, whimsical manner. It was childish; and people took it too seriously, and yet not seriously enough. A deep cleavage in his own life lay at the root of it. I wonder whether

---

[1] I have since learnt from Mr. A. W. Lawrence that this was a range constructed by their brother Frank in a disused clay-pit.

he himself ever knew why he did it, or rather had to do it.

As a private he once rang at the door of a field-marshal and asked the butler whether his master was in. He was not. Would he lunch at home? Yes. " Then tell his Lordship that Aircraftman Shaw will lunch with him."

One day in 1926 I met him at the gate of the British Museum in his private's uniform.

" Hullo, Lawrence."

" Do you recognize me? "

" Of course."

Then he said, " The whole afternoon I have been walking about the Museum where every attendant used to know me, and not a single one recognized me,[1] till I inquired about someone I missed. Then the man knew me." Quite so — what was the good of disguising if no one recognized him?

He was a man of genius, an immensely rich personality, a great artist; he suffered as few ever do, and he knew how much he suffered. " Go into the desert for a few years," he said, " and you will return a prophet. If you stay there too long, you will never speak again." Had he been born

---

[1] This was a craving for normality translated into the wish to appear indistinguishable. Cf. with the above, Lawrence's marginal remark in Mr. Graves's book (" T. E. Lawrence to Robert Graves," p. 71).

on the fringe of a desert he would have become a prophet. Had he lived in the Christian Middle Ages he would have become a saint. He had the instincts and negations of both, without their faith, and under modern conditions had to turn it all into an incomprehensible joke. When I saw him last, in 1930, I showed him a passage in my forthcoming book[1] and asked whether he objected. He did not. Here it is:

> There are men who crave for mortification, " *la mia allegrezza è la malinconia.*" But unless this desire assumes a standardized religious form — hair-shirt or hermit's hut — and can be represented as a profitable bargain for another world men dare not admit it, even to themselves. If proved beyond doubt it is described as madness. Educated men may become monks, but must not enlist as privates in the army.

There was a deep negation of life in him — " It were better there was nought." But he wished to believe that his mode of life was the result of his philosophy: " Trees grew down by the river, till they rose above its bank and saw the ruins of Troy, and they withered away."[2]

[1] " England in the Age of the American Revolution," pp. 93-4.
[2] On reading " The Letters of T. E. Lawrence " (p. 654) I found that this was a semi-quotation from a poem of F. L. Lucas.

It was this negation of life which drew him to the desert, and next to the sterility of garrison life. Besides, there was the infinite capacity for suffering, and even the downright desire for it. He could bear any pain, outride the Arabs on a camel, do without sleep and food; at times it almost seemed as if he had no physical existence.

He was small, but so well proportioned that, except by comparison, one hardly realized how undersized he was. He had sad, piercing eyes: his greatness was in them. He spoke in a low, soft voice. When he talked seriously, people would listen spellbound. He had style in talking and style in every line he wrote.

One night when I was with him he brought coal in a big sheet of brown paper and shoved it into the grate. The sheet caught fire. He was crouching by the fireplace and did not move an inch. He turned the blazing fringe upwards, looked at it for a moment, and then quietly blew it out, starting each time from the outer end, as if he were licking the flap of an envelope. He had first considered whether he still needed the paper and next, at one glance, realized the strategical position, that the flame travels quickest along the edge, and that by gently blowing it out towards the top you can stop it completely. I said that if I survived him I would tell that story. " You know too much Dostoievsky," he replied.

He was a great novel reader: I am not. One night, however, when I was bored, I asked him for a novel, a good novel. " But there must be no love story in it. Do you know such a novel? " He sat curled up in one of his big leather armchairs (he got them from a financier whom he had saved from a wrong investment in the Middle East). He thought for a moment. Then his face lit up, and he pointed to a manuscript on the table. " Yes, I know one. The Arab revolt. There is no love story in it, and that's why it succeeded. Take it." I carried away a few chapters, but don't know to which book they belonged, the one which vanished at Reading Railway Station (I can never quite swallow that story) or to " The Seven Pillars of Wisdom."

The thing which was wholly absent from Lawrence's mental make-up was a legal conception of fact or a mathematical idea of accuracy. He was fond of Cubist paintings, and his statements sometimes partook of a Cubist character. It was easy to arraign them on formal grounds, but if probed they would often be found to express the truth better than would a formally correct account. He never bothered or condescended to make his statements " foolproof." On one occasion he accused someone of having " packed a delegation." When afterwards I repeated to him a passionate denunciation of what he had said, he replied, " The man asked the delegation whether he might have some of his own friends present. He filled the room with them. There, people do not understand these nice distinctions. It was like a football game on an Irish village green; soon the entire village is playing. The room was packed, and that sufficed. In fact, the man afterwards boasted how clever he had been."

There was a stillness of soul in him and a pain that was timeless. And he disliked the precision of dates. He told me that in his History Finals at Oxford he spoke merely in centuries — " in the beginning of the twelfth " or " towards the end of the fifteenth century," etc. Only once he named a date — in brackets: " about the middle of the eleventh century (1066) . . ."

Lawrence was not happy outside England. He loved the English countryside, and was miserable when in 1926 he had to go with his regiment to India. He said he had finished with the East. He made the army his monastery. He wanted to be " like a brown paper parcel " and have no decisions to take. It was his penance. Some said that it was because the British Government had " let down the Arabs." This was nonsense. He never felt that way, and as adviser for Arab affairs to Mr. Churchill had full scope for working further on their behalf.[1] His penance was like that of the medieval monks, cosmic rather than individual. " For the sins of mankind " might have been the definition of a devout Roman Catholic, but he was neither a Catholic nor devout, and kept no accounts with Heaven. Still the instincts behind the penance were the same.

In the summer of 1930, when I was Political Secretary to the Jewish Agency for Palestine, I wanted to see and consult him. To secure a reply, I goaded him a bit, and asked why he continued to call on friends who were lords and generals but not on " ex-Private Namier." He replied:

> 338171 A/C Shaw
> R.A.F. Mount Batten
> Plymouth
> 15. VII. 30

DEAR NAMIER

Lords and Generals! They were long ago, I think : unless you mean the Plymouth ones, who see me (I am a local curio) when they come to Mount Batten.

I'm out of conceit with London, this year. It costs too much to get there: and camp is home now. Outside the fences I feel exposed and lonely.

[1] See below, pp. 303-304. Also " T. E. Lawrence to R. Graves," pp. 54, 77, and 181-83; and " T. E. Lawrence to Liddell Hart," pp. 144 and 160.

Yet, if you must see me, so be it. Must I come up, or can you get travelling expenses in coming down here? Plymouth is a filthy hole, where man is vile, but the salt sea glorious.

Take warning that I am eight years in the ranks now and by that much out of date in affairs. I read nothing, correspond with nobody and meet no one concerned in the wide world. So I'm a blind man to ask a direction of. Yet, as I say, what I am is wholly at your disposal. I can get off any midday of a Saturday, and am free till midnight of the Sunday. Here or there.[1]

Yours ever

T. E. SHAW

He widely differed from those who love the Arabs as a stick with which to beat the Jews; and was therefore pro-Zionist. In the ensuing talk which I had with him on July 19, 1930, he said — I took down his words in shorthand and read them back to him afterwards:

The problem of Zionism is the problem of the third generation.[2] It is the grandsons of your immigrants who will make it succeed or fail, but the odds are so much in its favour that the experiment is worth backing; and I back it not because of the

[1] The last three words are added in blue pencil.
[2] Cf. " T. E. Lawrence to Robert Graves," p. 114.

Jews, but because a regenerated Palestine is going to raise the whole moral and material status of its Middle East neighbours.

He was prepared to testify on behalf of Zionism to the Cabinet. I repeated the offer at the time to Mr. Malcolm MacDonald, but nothing came of it.

Among other things, Lawrence told me that day the story of the Cairo Conference of 1921, and how Transjordan had come to be separated from Palestine. I put down in a minute what I heard from him, and a funny story it was — Lawrence had a great sense of humour. But the time has not yet come to publish it and I give here the bare gist of it:

> The decisions of the Cairo Conference were prepared by us in London, over dinner tables at the Ship Restaurant in Whitehall. It was decided to include Transjordan in Palestine, to make it indistinguishable from Palestine, and to open it to Jewish immigration. Every point was decided at Cairo, as originally settled in London, except the one about Transjordan. When the Conference met, Abdulla was marching from the Hejaz to Transjordan with a view to attacking the French in Syria. To stop him would have required troops and money. It was decided to negotiate with him.
> There were three possibilities:

1. To keep a British garrison in Transjordan.

2. To establish there a native State under British direction.

3. To let the French have it.

As the Cabinet were absolutely opposed to British troops being sent across the Jordan and money being spent on operations, the first possibility was ruled out. Abdulla could therefore be stopped by persuasion only. Had he gone on against Syria, the French, after having dealt with them there, could not have been stopped from occupying Transjordan, which had been used as a base against them. Therefore the best solution was to have a " British Abdulla " in Transjordan. The situation which had arisen in the spring of 1921 left no other choice.

" And we had to foot the bill," I said.

" Yes," he replied, " you had to foot the bill. But you would have been no better off if the French had taken Transjordan."

And here are a few other scraps from that conversation:

" If you had four hundred decent British policemen in Palestine, there would be no problem." I asked whether that did not depend very much on who commanded them. He thought not. Policemen go about the country on their own and are not commanded.

About Ibn-Saud, he said that he was the last protest of the desert against Europe. He was a great man, but had no creative idea behind him. His work could not survive him. Such waves of reaction have come out of the interior of Arabia again and again.

Lawrence talked disparagingly about Pan-Islamism in politics. It is a fiction, and there is no more to it than there would be to a Pan-Christianity. There are at present at least nine Khalifs. Every Mohammedan ruler who has the power compels his people to accept him as Khalif. The bogy of the Khalifate was merely a weapon against the British Government and a means of self-aggrandizement, and its managers had to go lower and lower in that game. They started with the Sultan, next they tried the Emir of Afghanistan, now they might be capable of trying some Mufti, but it is a game which leads nowhere.

The British Government know little. When he wanted support for the Hejaz he made them believe that it was a great thing to have the Sherif of Mecca on our side. But that was mere bluff.

He told me a great deal about the future of the Jews in Palestine and of British rule in the East. About the Mesopotamia rebellion he said that it was due to British administrators having become accustomed during the war to numerous battalions. Only when we learn again how to rule without soldiers shall we be safe.

He was amused at the stories of his having been the " Uncrowned King of Arabia." In reality, he had been careful to keep in the background and usually gave his orders through Emir Feisul. Only a limited number of tribes knew and followed his person. Once a tribe sent word to Feisul that there was a railway bridge which they wished to blow up in order to derail and loot a military train, and asked that he should send them a " Lawrence." They thought that this was some kind of craft.

I never saw him after 1930. When I once asked him why he did not come to see me, he wrote on October 12, 1932:

> I came to London for a leave of a few days, carrying your letter of 6 ix. in my pocket. I hoped to get to Gloucester Walk and see you. But the powers were unkind. I had many worries, which took most of my day energies: and when the nights came I walked up and down the crowds, or looked at lights and listened to traffic, as a refuge against seeing people.

And in a later letter, " Sick of Plymouth . . . There is no place like London."

The last letter which I ever received from him he concluded by saying about a common friend: " It is sad to see a big man in retirement and not knowing what to do. I wish we could all die in harness."

"SEVEN PILLARS OF WISDOM"[1]

("*Manchester Guardian*," *July* 29, 1935)

LAWRENCE once talked to me about the kind of subscriber he wanted for the limited edition of the " Seven Pillars of Wisdom." " I have put Sir ——— ——— down for it; he will neither read nor sell it; to that extent it will be as if published posthumously." " But then why not leave it for posthumous publication? " I asked. No, he had to see it through the press himself, to choose the paper, the type, the binding, and the illustrations. The dress provided for books was to him a subject of intense, absorbing interest, and so lavish was he over the " Seven Pillars " that the returns of its thirty-guinea edition did not repay the cost of production. To cover the balance he had to publish " The Revolt in the Desert," which he described to me as a " Boy Scout Edition " — compared to the other it was a book of trivial adventure.

But how to write about the " Seven Pillars of Wisdom "? One could discuss chapters of history or strategy, the beauty of the style, the

[1] " Seven Pillars of Wisdom," by T. E. Lawrence.

narrative and its sustained interest, the flashes of quiet humour or of whimsical wisdom, and the descriptions so vivid or plastic. But none of this is of its core; a mind and life break through the pages of the book with a stark directness such as few writers would dare, or be able, to achieve. Here was a human being of rare texture, with a spirit, a will, and an understanding which were almost uncanny; but in chains, invisible chains, for which he sought an equivalent in actual life, yearning at the same time for a white peace and endless freedom. He was fastidious, highly educated, sophisticated; but pain, the fear and love and fascination of pain, made him into an ascetic. Under conditions which answered his nature, he broke through the fetters and became a spirit let adrift and " given licence in strange airs "; he saw over the crest into " the emptiness of open spaces."

In the desert he found men " geographically beyond temptation," on whom there was " the mark of nomadism, that most deep and biting social discipline "; who " found luxury in abnegation, renunciation, self-restraint," " made nakedness of the mind as sensuous as nakedness of the body," and saved their souls in a hard selfishness — " dry souls ready to be set on fire."

Lawrence once said to me about the Semites: " To the end of the world will they go for loot, but if an idea crosses their path, they forget the loot and follow the idea." He went to them carrying an idea —

> I drew these tides of men into my hands
> And wrote my will across the sky in stars.

Here is his description of the men:

> Their mind was strange and dark, full of depressions and exaltations, lacking in rule, but with more of ardour and more fertile in belief than any other in the world. . . . They were as unstable as water, and, like water, would perhaps finally prevail. Since the dawn of life in successive waves they had been dashing themselves against the coasts of flesh. . . . One such wave (and not the least) I raised and rolled before the breath of an idea till it reached its crest and toppled over and fell at Damascus.

Everything that mattered in him was of the spirit and had to retranslate itself into thought or art. In the " Seven Pillars " he found self-expression and created a deathless thing. After that there was nothing but a lingering life and grey suffering, and his only escape into freedom was speed, deadly speed.

Lawrence believed — I do not know on what grounds or with how much justification — that Doughty had gone to Arabia mainly in search of " copy " on which to practise a new style of

writing ; and we talked with regret about
Napoleon having wasted his years in St. Helena
other man ever had. But then Napoleon was a
on a purpose, when he had copy such as no
man of action, pragmatic, with a warped per-
ception and insufficient sincerity of thought.
Lawrence (at least in his own consciousness and
tastes) was not a man of action — " I hated responsibility . . . and . . . in all my life objects
had been gladder to me than persons, and ideas
than objects." " I felt mean, to fill the place of a
man of action; for my standards of value were
a wilful reaction against theirs, and I despised
their happiness." And this was his " reaction
against success ":

> In the blank light of victory we could
> scarcely identify ourselves. We spoke with
> surprise, sat emptily, fingered upon our
> white skirts . . . to-day each man owned
> his desire so utterly that he was fulfilled in it
> and became meaningless.

His strategy faithfully reflected his innermost
mind and being ; and he discerned its principles
in perfect clarity during an illness aggravated by
an incident of which the horror is stamped upon
his book and story. Lawrence never shirked
pain, and did not regard it highly in others ; but
he shunned inflicting mental torment, and he

loathed killing. However, in extraordinary circumstances he had to execute a man who had done murder, and whom he ordered to stand up while he shot him at close range. In the crisis of his haunted illness he developed a theory of campaign, almost unwilling to admit that homicide is occasionally permissible in warfare:

> In Turkey things were scarce and precious, men less esteemed than equipment. . . . The death of a Turkish bridge or rail, machine or gun or charge of high explosive was more profitable to us than the death of a Turk. In the Arab Army at the moment we were chary both of materials and of men. Governments saw men only in mass ; but our men, being irregulars, were not formations but individuals. An individual death, like a pebble dropped in water, might make but a brief hole ; yet rings of sorrow widened out therefrom. We could not afford casualties.

> The Turks were stupid ; the Germans behind them dogmatical. They would believe that rebellion was absolute, like war, and deal with it on the analogy of war. Analogy in human things was fudge, anyhow ; and war upon rebellion was messy and slow, like eating soup with a knife.

> Battles in Arabia were a mistake, since we profited by them only by the ammunition

the enemy fired off. . . . We had nothing material to lose, so our best line was to defend nothing and to shoot nothing.

. . . suppose we were . . . an influence, an idea, a thing intangible, invulnerable, without front or back, drifting about like a gas ? Armies were like plants, immobile, firm-rooted, nourished through long stems to the head. We might be a vapour, blowing where we listed. Our kingdom lay in each man's mind. . . .

. . . the preaching was victory and the fighting a delusion. . . .

Lawrence, in his almost " disbodied " existence, had a sway over men, most often exercised imperceptibly ; but at times he would pronounce words which fell " like a sword in their midst." Material action he despised. When in January 1918 he won a complete victory, inflicting heavy losses on the Turks at a cost of only twenty or thirty killed on his side, he felt that the " destruction of this thousand poor Turks would not affect the issue of the war " ; " this evening there was no glory left, but the terror of the broken flesh, which had been our own men, carried past us to their homes." He sat down and wrote a report, which he sent over to the British headquarters in Palestine " for the Staff's consumption ":

It was meanly written for effect, full of
quaint smiles and mock simplicities ; and
made them think me a modest amateur, doing his best after the great models ; not a
clown, leering after them where they with
Foch, bandmaster, at their head went drum-
ming down the old road of effusion of blood
into the house of Clausewitz. Like the
battle, it was a nearly-proof parody of regu-
lation use. Headquarters loved it, and inno-
cently, to crown the jest, offered me a
decoration on the strength of it.

The " Seven Pillars," written in a style and
imagery seldom surpassed or even equalled, will
live as a work of art, far greater than Lawrence's
material achievements. Take this description of
a street in Jeddah as an example of his mastery
of language :

The style of architecture was like crazy
Elizabethan half-timber work, in the elaborate Cheshire fashion, but gone gimcrack to
an incredible degree. House-fronts were
fretted, pierced and pargetted till they
looked as though cut out of cardboard for a
romantic stage-setting. Every storey jutted,
every window leaned one way or other ;
often the very walls sloped. It was like a
dead city, so clean underfoot, and so quiet.
Its winding, even streets were floored with
damp sand solidified by time and as silent to

the tread as any carpet. The lattices and wall-
returns deadened all reverberation of voice.
There were no carts, nor any streets wide
enough for carts, no shod animals, no bustle
anywhere. Everything was hushed, strained,
even furtive. The doors of houses shut
softly as we passed.

Or watch these pictures — of such there are
hundreds :

> . . . the searchlights began slowly to tra-
> verse the plain in complex intersections,
> drawing pencils of wheeling light across the
> flats. . . .

> We rode gently . . . through a thin
> shower of rain which came slanting strangely
> and beautifully across the sunlight.

> The camp gradually stilled as the tired
> men and animals went one by one to sleep ;
> a white mist collected softly over them, and
> in it the fires became slow pillars of smoke.

> . . . it was a good song, with a rhyth-
> mical beat which the camels loved, so that
> they put down their heads, stretched their
> necks out far, and with lengthened pace
> shuffled forward musingly while it lasted.

Or take this account given of himself in an argument with Arabs:

When I am angry I pray God to swing our globe into the fiery sun and prevent the sorrows of the not-yet-born ; but when I am content I want to lie for ever in the shade till I become a shade myself.

Or mark the quaint wisdom of the following sentence about Feisul:

He never gave a partial decision, nor a decision so impracticably just that it must lead to disorder.

Or this impression of Feisul:

His eyelids were dropped, and his black beard and colourless face were like a mask against the strange, still watchfulness of his body.

Or see what a picture Lawrence can draw of a man in a few lines:

. . . the flesh of his face was torn away by smallpox. From its white ruin two restless eyes looked out, very bright and big; for the faintness of his eyelashes and eyebrows made his stare directly disconcerting. . . . His manner . . . was abrupt, indeed imperious; with a humour as cracked as his cackling laugh.

And, finally, read this about a battlefield covered with the stripped bodies of Turks:

The dead men looked wonderfully beautiful. The night was shining gently down, softening them into new ivory. Turks were white-skinned on their clothed parts, much whiter than the Arabs; and these soldiers had been very young. Close round them lapped the dark wormwood, now heavy with dew, in which the ends of the moonbeams sparkled like sea-spray. The corpses seemed flung so pitifully on the ground, huddled anyhow in low heaps. Surely if straightened they would be comfortable at last. So I put them all in order, one by one, very wearied myself, and longing to be of these quiet ones, not of the restless, noisy, aching mob up the valley, quarrelling over the plunder, boasting of their speed and strength to endure God knew how many toils and pains of this sort ; with death, whether we won or lost, waiting to end the history.

HIS LETTERS

("*Manchester Guardian,*" *January* 7, 1939)

Books will be written on the basis of this book,[1] but it is well-nigh impossible to review it. Here are some 600 letters selected from a much larger collection, which itself necessarily represents only a fraction of the letters written by Lawrence. " I hate letter-writing "; " letter-writing is a vice "; and so he wrote innumerable letters which were discourses and disquisitions rather than missives of an informative or a business character. Their range is wide and they have no focus, not even that of a diary, which is self-centred. The story of Lawrence's life could be followed up in these letters, his work and interests, his relations to people, his views on art, literature, architecture, his style, and so on. Here I propose to deal with one psychological aspect only: Lawrence's pursuit of an indefinable, disbodied self and its direct expression divorced from matter, and of its despairing counterpart in his enlisting as a private.

[1] " The Letters of T. E. Lawrence," edited by David Garnett.

There was a yearning in him for the peace of
empty spaces, for the great void where nothing
obstructs the spirit, for the plain, and still more
for the desert. He wrote in 1908, at the age of
twenty:

> . . . a mountain may be a great thing, a
> grand thing, but . . . a plain is the best
> country: the purifying influence is the
> paramount one in a plain . . . one feels the
> littleness of things, of details, and the great
> and unbroken level of peacefulness of the
> whole. . . .

Ten years later he thus explained the attraction
which Arabia had for him:

> It is the old, old civilisation, which has
> refined itself clear of household gods and
> half the trappings which ours hastens to
> assume. The gospel of bareness in materials
> is a good one, and it involves apparently a
> sort of moral bareness too (July 15, 1918).
> . . . the Arab East to me is always an
> empty place. . . . (October 27, 1922.)
> . . . had the world been mine I'd have left
> out animal life upon it. (June 27, 1923.)

Correlated to this negation of the material and
of life itself was a straining and wrestling for direct
expression. This is Lawrence's description of

a stained-glass window in Rheims Cathedral
(August 29, 1910):

> . . . an . . . adorable mist of orange and
> red . . . a maze of colours, blended to de-
> spair, without a suspicion of pattern or form
> in it. . . . It is pure colour, perfect.

Poetry was to him " the crown and head, the only
essential branch of letters "; but even there he
found a mere " collection of bonbons " when he
" wanted a meal." He wrote about the " Seven
Pillars of Wisdom " (October 23, 1922):

> I can't write poetry: so in prose I aimed
> at providing a meal for the fellow-seekers
> with myself. For this the whole experience,
> and emanations and surroundings . . . of a
> man are necessary. Whence the many facets
> of my book. . . .
> . . . It's too elaborate and conscious a con-
> struction to admit simplicity. . . . Yet I felt
> that I could reach the static by very exercise
> of this fault. Will can only be expressed by
> activity: thought exists for others only when
> it comes out in words: so I could transfuse
> my feelings, by putting them into a gesture,
> a conversation, and sunset or noon-day-heat,
> or even into the cadences of vowels and con-
> sonants which made up a phrase.

A year later he wrote:

299

. . . lately I have been finding my deepest satisfaction in the collocation of words so ordinary and plain that they cannot mean anything to a book-jaded mind: and out of some of such I can draw deep stuff. It is perhaps that certain sequences of vowels or consonants imply more than others: that writing of this sort has music in it?

There is even a pattern in these sequences which seem " to impose themselves through the eye alone."

But action and the attempt at self-expression in art alike left Lawrence deeply dissatisfied. In the later stages " the Arab Adventure got rather too black and heavy and the gaiety died out," and before the end was reached " all my thought was of going home, where I meant to get transferred to the French front." And he writes thus about his book:

I thought that the mind I had (and I've matched it competitively often against other fellows, and have an opinion of it), if joined to a revival of the war-passion, would sweep over the ordinary rocks of technique. So I got into my garret, and in that month . . . excited myself with hunger and cold and sleeplessness more than did de Quincey with his opium. It gave me the foundation, and on that I worked . . . biting the lines

deeper. . . . I had hopes all the while that
it was going to be a big thing. . . . I sent it
to the printer, and when it came back in a
fresh shape I saw that it was no good.
(August 26, 1922.)

I went through four versions in the four
years I struggled with it, and I gave it all
my nights and days till I was nearly blind
and mad. The failure of it was mainly what
broke my nerve, and sent me into the R.A.F.
(February 20, 1924.)

Lawrence scrutinized the book, loved and
hated it, like his own person; was eager to learn
other people's reaction to it, and found praise
harder to bear than criticism. His self-deprecia-
tion made him writhe at success which merely
heightened his inward feeling of failure:

If my success had not been so great, and
so easy, I would despise it less: and when
to my success in action was added (according
to those whose judgment I asked) success in
book-writing, also at first venture — why,
then I broke down, and ran here to hide
myself. (May 30, 1923.)

He loathed barrack life. " So because my senses
hate it, my will forces me to it . . . and a comfortable life would seem now to me sinful."

. . . I'm afraid (physically afraid) of other

301

men: their animal spirits seem to me the most terrible companions to haunt a man: and I hate their noise. (November 12, 1922.)

These are foul-mouthed, and behind their mouths is a pervading animality of spirit, whose unmixed bestiality frightens me and hurts me. (May 14, 1923.)

A filthy business all of it, and yet . . . These fellows are the reality, and you and I, the selves who used to meet in London and talk of fleshless things, are only the outward wrappings of a core like these fellows. (March 27, 1923.)

Lawrence gave various explanations of why he had enlisted and why he insisted on remaining in the ranks, and knew that none of them was satisfactory:

Honestly, I couldn't tell you exactly why I joined up: though the night before I did . . . I sat up and wrote out all the reasons I could see or feel in myself for it. But they came to little more than that it was a necessary step, forced on me by an inclination towards ground-level: by a despairing hope that I'd find myself on common ground with men: by a little wish to make myself a little more human than I had become in Barton Street: by an itch to make myself ordinary in a mob of likes: also I'm broke, so far as money goes, by an unexpected event. All these are reasons: but unless they are cumulative they are miserably inadequate. I wanted to join up, that's all. . . . (November 12, 1922.)

Regard it as an asylum for the little-spirited. . . . I want not to be big any more. (December 20, 1923.)

. . . self-degradation is my aim. . . . (March 19, 1923.)

The most trivial explanation with which he would sometimes try to fob off people, or even himself, was that he had joined up in search of fresh material for a book. But for the one explanation which has attained the widest currency, that he enlisted to " do penance " for the British Government having " let down " the Arabs, there is not one shred of evidence in Lawrence's letters or writings; on the contrary — he wrote about Mr. Winston Churchill and his settlement in a " Draft Preface " to the " Seven Pillars of Wisdom," dated November 18, 1922:

He executed the whole McMahon undertaking (called a treaty by some who have not seen it) for Palestine, for Trans-Jordania, and for Arabia. In Mesopotamia he went far beyond its provisions. . . .

I do not wish . . . to make long explanations: but must put on record my conviction that England is out of the Arab affair with clean hands. Some Arab advocates (the most vociferous joined our ranks after the Armistice) have rejected my judgment on this point. Like a tedious Pensioner I showed them my wounds (over sixty I have, each scar evidence of a pain incurred in Arab service) as proof I had worked sincerely on their side. They found me out-of-date: and I was happy to withdraw from a political milieu which had never been congenial.

And again in a letter to Professor Yale, dated October 22, 1929:

It is my deliberate opinion that the Winston Churchill settlement of 1921–22 (in which I shared) honourably fulfils the whole of the promises we made to the Arabs, in so far as the so-called British spheres are concerned. . . .

. . . Winston's settlement so pleased me that I withdrew wholly from politics, with clean hands, I think, and enlisted in the Air Force. . . .